Food, Fuel, and Shelter

Other Titles in this Series

The Changing Economics of World Energy, edited by Bernhard J. Abrahamsson

Indonesia's Oil, Sevinc Carlson

Desertification: Environmental Degradation in and around Arid Lands, edited by Michael H. Glantz

The Nuclear Impact: A Case Study of the Plowshare Program to Produce Natural Gas by Underground Nuclear Stimulation in the Rocky Mountains, Frank Kreith and Catherine B. Wrenn

Natural Resources for a Democratic Society: Public Participation in Decision-Making, edited by Albert Utton, W. R. Derrick Sewell, and Timothy O'Riordan

Social Assessment Manual: A Guide to the Preparation of the Social Well-Being Account for Planning Water Resource Projects, Stephen J. Fitzsimmons, Lorrie I. Stuart, and Peter C. Wolff

Water Needs for the Future: Political, Economic, Legal, and Technological Issues in a National and International Framework, edited by Ved P. Nanda

Environmental Effects of Complex River Development: International Experience, edited by Gilbert F. White

Food from the Sea, Frederick W. Bell

The Geopolitics of Energy, Melvin A. Conant and Fern Racine Gold

EARTHCARE: Global Protection of Natural Areas, edited by Edmund A. Schofield

Water in a Developing World: The Management of a Critical Resource, edited by Albert E. Utton and Ludwik A. Teclaff

Conservation and the Changing Direction of Economic Growth, edited by Bernhard J. Abrahamsson

Westview Special Studies in Natural Resources and Energy Management

Food, Fuel, and Shelter: A Watershed Analysis of Land-Use Trade-Offs in a Semi-Arid Region
Timothy D. Tregarthen

As human pressures on land intensify, land-use decisions in response to the new demands become increasingly critical. Thus, the fate of the little-known Running Creek Watershed assumes a broad importance. Running Creek Watershed is a 150-kilometer strip of land lying just east of the rapidly expanding urban corridor of Colorado's front range. The land in the watershed is devoted primarily to the production of food, and includes pasture, dry crop, and irrigated crop operations. Two sources of demand suggest dramatic future changes in this land-use pattern: advancing urbanization, and energy demands for the coal available in a large deposit 25 kilometers east of Denver.

In this volume Timothy Tregarthen presents a synthesis of discussions and papers presented at a 1976 conference that focused on the trade-offs implicit in the land-use alternatives of food production, urbanization, and energy development. Sponsored by the Wright-Ingraham Institute, the conference brought together a wide range of scientists, humanists, public officials, representatives of industrial and agricultural organizations, and interested citizens concerned not only about this important regional problem, but about the broader implications of competing land-use needs. Conference participants examined factors important to changes in land use, giving particular attention to the natural, economic, political, and value systems at work on the watershed in terms of how these systems affect and will be affected by changing land-use patterns.

Timothy D. Tregarthen is associate professor and chairman of the Department of Economics at the University of Colorado, Colorado Springs, and a member of the Wright-Ingraham Institute's board of advisory consultants. He served as director of the Food, Fuel, and Shelter conference and has taught in the institute's Integrative Studies program since its inception in 1973.

Report of a conference on the
Front Range of Colorado

May 20-22, 1976
Greeley, Colorado

Wright-Ingraham Institute
Colorado Springs, Colorado

Food, Fuel, and Shelter
A Watershed Analysis of Land-Use Trade-Offs in a Semiarid Region

Timothy D. Tregarthen

Routledge
Taylor & Francis Group
LONDON AND NEW YORK

First published 1978 by Westview Press

Published 2018 by Routledge
52 Vanderbilt Avenue, New York, NY 10017
2 Park Square, Milton Park, Abingdon, Oxon OX14 4RN

Routledge is an imprint of the Taylor & Francis Group, an informa business

Library of Congress Number: 77-19355

ISBN 13: 978-0-367-02043-9 (hbk)
ISBN 13: 978-0-367-1730-1 (pbk)

TABLE OF CONTENTS

PREFACE

Land use decisions are becoming increasingly critical as human pressures on land intensify. The arrangement, as well as the nature, of human activity with respect to land and the resources it represents shape the destiny of the human race. A conference devoted to land use questions on a little known watershed on the eastern plains of Colorado thus assumes more general importance, focusing on the kinds of choices that must be made all over the world in allocating land for man's needs for food, fuel, and shelter. The conference, which this report documents, addressed the trade-offs among these uses in a rural area that now provides food, includes coal deposits that could provide energy, and lies in the path of the shelter needs of urban development.

The conference, titled "Food, Fuel, and Shelter: Choices for the Future on Running Creek (Box Elder) Watershed," was held May 20-22, 1976 at the University of Northern Colorado at Greeley. Funded in part by the Colorado Humanities Program, the conference had additional support from Cameron Engineers, Inc., the Colorado State Land Use Commission, E. D'Appolonia Consulting Engineers, Inc., Elbert County, the National Science Foundation, Public Service Company of Colorado, the Pueblo Regional Planning Commission, Rocky Mountain Energy Company, and Environment Consultants, Inc. Additional funding for the publication of this report has been provided by the National Endowment for the Humanities and Public Service Company of Colorado.

Participants at the conference divided into three working groups, each considering the impacts of one of the three major development forms — food production, energy development, and urbanization — facing the watershed. These groups also sought to identify the factors that would influence changes in land use. Participants reassembled in plenary sessions at intervals throughout the three day meeting to share results of individual sessions, to hear guest speakers, and to revise methodological strategies. A list of participants of the conference, together with a schedule of sessions and speakers, is provided on page 98.

This report is based on the discussions and presentations at the conference. It relies on the background papers prepared by leaders of the working groups. These group leaders included Victor Hornbein, Denver architect; William Lord, University of Colorado, Boulder economist; Alan Merson of the University of Denver, College of Law and Chairman of the Colorado Land Commission; Eldon Stevens, philosopher at the University of Colorado, Colorado Springs; George Van Dyne, systems ecologist at Colorado State University, Fort Collins; and David Ver Steeg of Environment Consultants, Inc., Denver and Colorado School of Mines, Golden. Early drafts of this report have been reviewed by each of the group leaders, and by F. Martin Brown, John Hand, Thomas McKee, James Miller, Gayle Packard-Seeburger, and Eli Yakich. Footnotes in the text indicate sections which rely heavily on material in the background papers, presentations made at the conference, or other materials. References cited in the background papers are listed in the Bibliography. In addition, a glossary of technical terms is provided on page 102. Finally, conversion factors relating the metric measures used in the text to perhaps more familiar measures such as acres, bushels, and miles are given on page 100.

The conference sought to bring together a diverse group of individuals to discuss implications of alternative land use choices for an environmental unit which represents many of the most critical choices facing society today. It sought also the production of a methodological framework in which those choices and the trade-offs they represent could be compared. The success of the conference in meeting these goals owes much to the efforts of the group leaders listed above. A special note of thanks goes to the organizations which provided financial support for the meeting. William Hynes, then the director of the Colorado Humanities Program, provided much helpful advice in planning the conference. Elizabeth Wright Ingraham, Director of the Wright-Ingraham Institute, has long been a vital force in pressing for integrated research efforts applied to land use problems in the region; her vision provided the initial impetus for this study. Brendan Doyle, also of the Institute, acted as coordinator of the conference; he, more than anyone else, put it together. Catherine Ingraham, John Torborg, and Frank Miller all added to the Institute's enormous contribution to the conference. Marion Philippusand Ruth Harris helped prepare the manuscript. William Sheehan designed and completed the final layout of the book. Conference photographs were taken by Lester LaForce, Denver; additional photographs were provided by Andrew Taylor, Colorado Springs. Finally, the participants of the conference, with their enthusiasm and talent, provided the lively discussion and provocative viewpoints on which this report largely relies. This has been very much a shared effort, one that I gratefully acknowledge.

T.D.T.
Colorado Springs, Colorado
June, 1977

INVESTIGATORY TEAM

Victor Hornbein, Architect
Victor Hornbein & Associates
Denver, Colorado

William Lord, Ph.D., Economics
Institute of Behavorial Sciences
University of Colorado
Boulder, Colorado

Alan Merson, LL.D.
College of Law, University of Denver
Chairman, Colorado Land Use Commission
Denver, Colorado

Eldon Stevens, Ph.D., Philosophy
University of Colorado
Colorado Springs, Colorado

Timothy D. Tregarthen, Ph.D., Economics (Conference Director)
University of Colorado
Colorado Springs, Colorado

George M. Van Dyne, Ph.D., Ecology
Colorado State University
Fort Collins, Colorado

David Ver Steeg
Environment Consultants, Inc.
Lakewood, Colorado

Brendan G. Doyle, (Conference Coordinator)
Wright-Ingraham Institute
Colorado Springs, Colorado

SPONSOR

Wright-Ingraham Institute
Colorado Springs, Colorado

CO-SPONSORS

Cameron Engineers Inc., Denver
Colorado Humanities Program, Boulder
Colorado Land Use Commission
E. D'Appolonia Consulting Engineers Inc., Denver and Pittsburgh, Pa.
Elbert County Land Use Administration
National Endowment for the Humanities, Washington D.C.
Public Service Company of Colorado, Denver
Pueblo Regional Planning Commission, Pueblo
Rocky Mountain Energy Company, Denver
Environment Consultants, Inc., Lakewood

PARTICIPATING AGENCIES, GROUPS AND FIRMS

Adams County, Planning Department
Arapahoe County, Planning Department
Charles F. Kettering Foundation, Dayton, Ohio
Colorado Association for Housing and Building, Denver
Colorado Farm Bureau, Denver
Colorado State Department of Local Affairs, Division of Planning
National Science Foundation, Washington, D.C.
Rocky Mountain Farmers' Union, Denver
University of Colorado, Denver, Urban and Regional Planning Program
USDA, Soil Conservation Service
Weld County, Planning Department

PRODUCTION STAFF

Brendan G. Doyle, editor
Ruth Harris, typist
Les LaForce, photographer
Marion Philippus, typist
William Sheehan, graphics
Andrew Taylor, photographer

"Culture is not measured by the greatness of the field which is covered by our knowledge, but by the nicety with which we can perceive relations in that field, whether great or small."

Robert Louis Stevenson,
The Amateur Immigrant, 1896

CHAPTER ONE

THE WATERSHED: A METHODOLOGICAL OVERVIEW

Changing Perspectives: From Globe to Watershed

In January 1975, the Wright-Ingraham Institute sponsored a workshop which sought to examine the interrelationships of food, people, environment, and climate as they related to global prospects for the year 2000. The 20 scientists and educators who participated in this "Query into the Quarter Century" workshop focused on the enormous global challenge of providing for an increase in population in the next 25 years that may equal the total number of people that lived in the previous 40,000. Their conclusion was cautiously optimistic; it is at least possible that the demands for food, fuel, and shelter that this surge in population implies can be met — assuming careful resource management, moderating energy demands, and a fair amount of climatological luck.

The global concerns addressed at the Quėry workshop are of unquestioned importance. The survival of much — and conceivably all — of the human race depends on their successful resolution. But decisions ultimately relevant to global problems are typically faced not globally, but rather are taken up at somewhat more local levels — ranging from regional marketplaces to national governments. It was, therefore, appropriate to shift the focus of examination of the concerns of the Query workshop from the planet as a whole

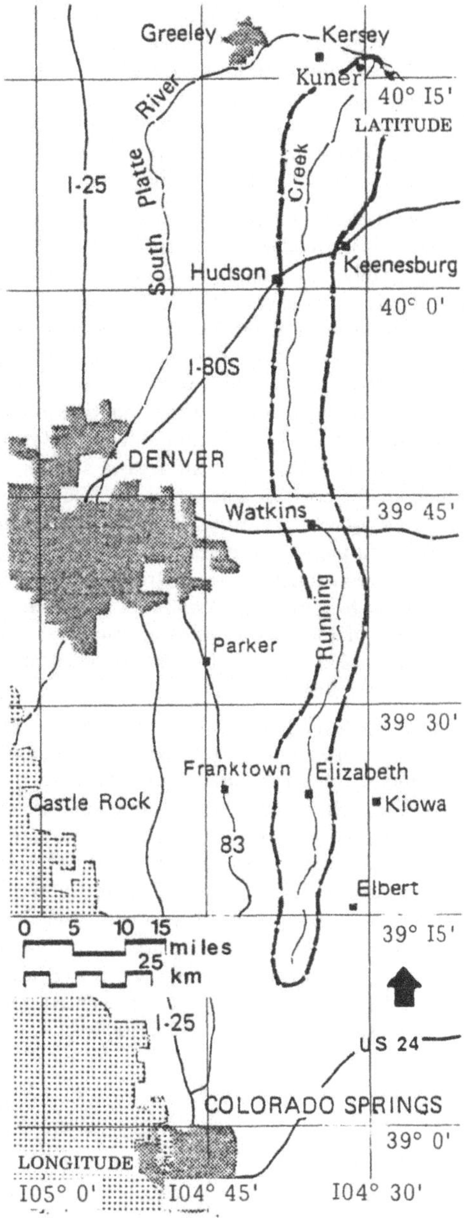

Fig. 1.1 Location of the Running Creek (Box Elder) Watershed

* The northern half of the creek is called Box Elder Creek, hence the reference to the Running Creek (Box Elder) watershed. For convenience, it shall be referred to below as the Running Creek Watershed. Names change approximately 19 km north of the town of Elizabeth.

to a specific region of it — in this case, the Running Creek (Box Elder) Watershed on Colorado's Front Range Piedmont.* The headwaters of Running Creek are located northeast of Colorado Springs; the creek flows north some 150 kilometers to drain into the South Platte River near Greeley. The watershed itself averages about eight kilometers in width (see map, Fig. 1.1).

The Running Creek Watershed does not rank high in most agendas of concern about man's continuing ability to provide the food, fuel, and shelter requisite to a decent life. The watershed is rural (population about 5,000) in a nation that is largely urban. It is on the high plains half of a state noted for its mountains. It is an environmental unit in an age in which political boundaries are the focus of attention. But the watershed offers, in its relatively small area, a striking example of the critical choices that must be faced in the next quarter century. It has coal — lignite deposits suitable for gasification and readily available for consumption in metropolitan Denver. Proximity to a major metropolitan area increases the value of the region's mineral source, and suggests an added pressure for development on the watershed — urbanization.

Energy development and urbanization each suggest a conversion of land use from the present predominantly agricultural use of the watershed. The choices faced here in allocating land are representative of similar choices facing a wide range of areas in the interior West and, indeed, throughout the world. The watershed thus provides a local correlate of the global concerns of the Query workshop, and is an excellent area for study and analysis. The region may be termed pre-critical in that it faces, but has not yet experienced, rapid and intensive development of its resources.

Running Creek

Evolution of the Inquiry

The Wright-Ingraham Institute has been focusing attention on the Running Creek watershed for the past four years. Running Creek Field Station, site of the Institute's developing university program, experimental work, and climatological monitoring, is located in the southern quarter of the watershed. Operating from this base, the Institute has for the past five years sponsored the annual *Grasslands Seminar*, to which all watershed residents are invited for discussions, lectures, and demonstrations relevant to the area. Other annual events at the Field Station include *Naturalists Day* and the *Architects on the Plains Seminars*.

In 1972, a team of investigators, representing three Front Range universities and two private firms, began to examine methodologies for assessing land use alternatives on the watershed. This team organized an advisory group to guide the Institute's land use research. This group, which included representatives of local and state agencies involved in land use policy for the watershed, held meetings on a wide range of issues of regional concern, including coal development, drought planning, rural electrification, and solid waste disposal. These meetings, in addition to providing valuable information, continued to provide a focus on the watershed as a unit.

In tandem with meetings of the land use research advisory group, Institute staff members continued the gathering of data and mapping of the watershed. Some preliminary econometric work was done on determinants of land values near the town of Elizabeth, located on the watershed north of Running Creek Field Station.

In 1975, the Institute assembled an expanded team to continue the land use research effort. This group decided that it would be valuable to conduct a conference dealing with land use issues facing the watershed. The goal of the conference was to bring together scientists, humanists, representatives of public agencies and private firms, and interested citizens to examine the nature of the trade-offs implied by likely alternative land uses for the watershed.

The choice of land uses on which to focus was straightforward. The present dominant use was an obvious one — agriculture. Watershed agricultural operations consist primarily of grazing livestock, dryland farming, and irrigated farming. Second, coals of the Denver Basin represent a major exploitable resource; much of the watershed could be affected by the mining of these coals. Finally, the watershed parallels a developing urban corridor which some observers think may someday become a continuous metropolitian area, stretching over 200 miles from Cheyenne, Wyoming to Pueblo, Colorado. Bounded on the

Elizabeth Wright Ingraham

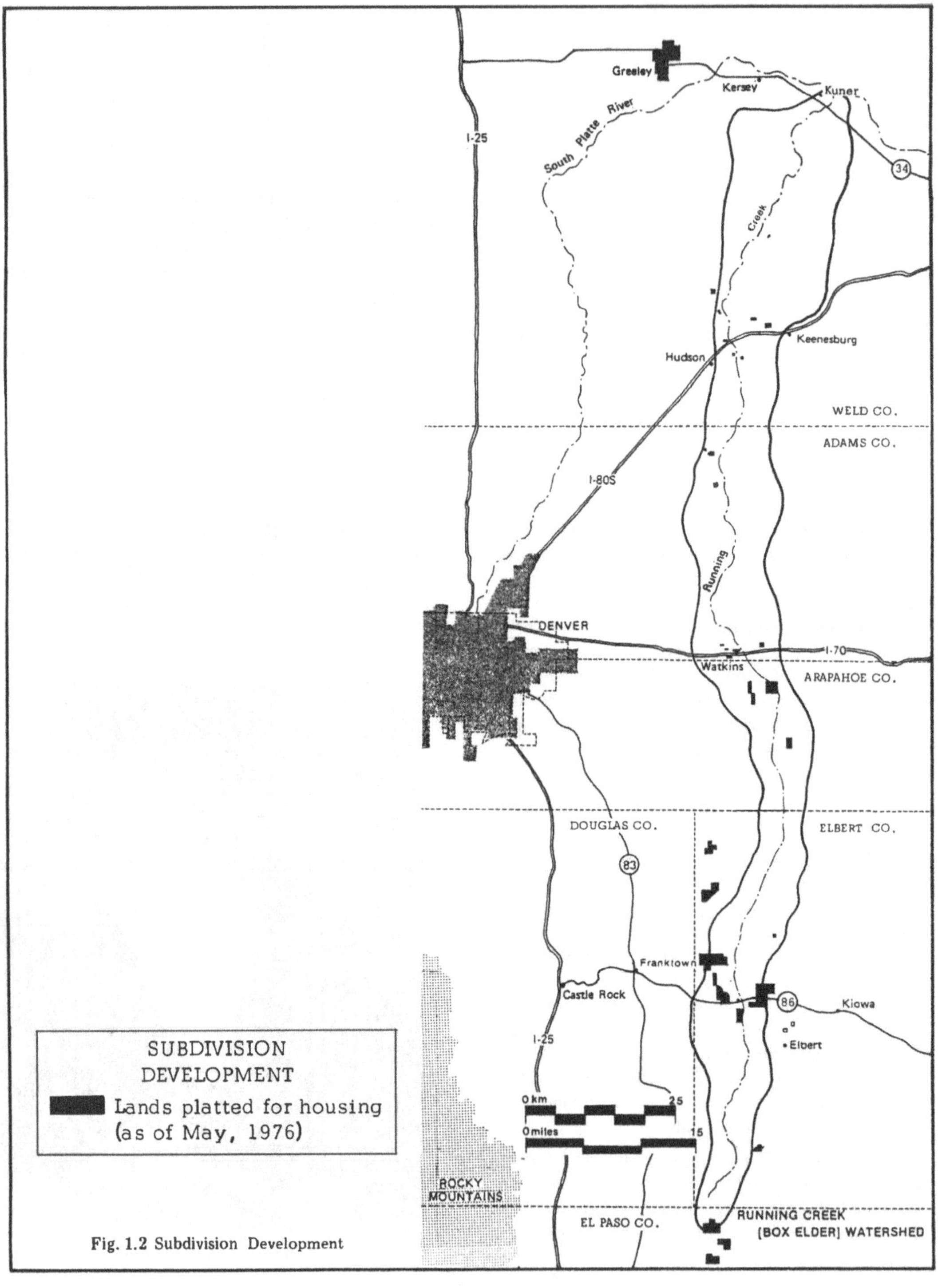

Fig. 1.2 Subdivision Development

west by the front range, lateral development of this corridor will inevitably put pressure on the watershed. Indeed, sub-division development is already occurring at an increasing rate, as suggested in Fig. 1.2. This prospect of increased urbanization, or perhaps suburbanization, was thus added as the "shelter" alternative development form.

Food production, energy development, and urbanization thus emerged as the three major land use demands to be considered. Each of these demands could be expected to influence the other two; it was the identification of the nature of these influences and the resultant trade-offs that the team hoped would emerge from discussions at the conference. Each of these demands — food, fuel, and shelter — was to be considered in terms of its impact on the region's natural economic, political, and social resources. The identification of these impacts for any one development form was then to be extended to a consideration of their significance for the other two. For example, the surface mining of coal would have a significant effect on the region's natural resources, which would in turn influence food production and urbanization.

Elizabeth, Colorado

Systems Analysis and the Analysis of Systems

The inquiry was thus to be a broad one. The focus on an environmental unit forced the crossing not only of political boundaries but of academic ones as well. The problem orientation of the investigation clearly dictated an interdisciplinary systems approach. An economic analysis of the region would be useful, as would a biological study of watershed plant species. But taken individually, they could not begin to address adequately the nature of the trade-offs implied by the alternatives of agricultural production, energy development, and urbanization.

"Systems approach" is a phrase as slippery in meaning as it is fashionable; it must therefore be defined with care. A system can be viewed as an organization or structure that functions in a particular way. This structure must be carefully bounded so that it is clear what is and is not included in it. One might, for example, consider a system to be an electric lamp. Electricity supplied to the lamp would then be viewed as a power source external to the system. Humans using the lamp would be similarly viewed as external decision makers. Such a view of this relatively simple system would be useful for one interested, say, in the repair of lamps. But if the question of interest were the demands made on the lamp, then the boundaries of the system would be extended to include human decision makers.

One can get quickly carried away in extending the arbitrarily selected boundaries of a system. An interest in demands made for lighting in general would involve the phenomenon of peak demand periods and might necessitate the inclusion of the economic, political, and social systems in terms of their impacts on the preferences and work schedules of individuals. And, of course, one could go as easily in the other direction, examining supply considerations for the power sources necessary for lighting.

The ultimate system, presumably, is the universe. And with a little thought, it is easy to extend the lamp example just described to this largest scale (a fundamental principle common to economics and ecology — that everything affects everything else — is useful in this exercise). But analyses that are zealously comprehensive in including all possible elements tend to be disastrously unwieldly in their application. One must economize on the thoroughness of one's coverage.

A system, then, should be defined with a view toward manageability of the work and the objectives of the analysis. Considered as a system, the Running Creek Watershed satisfies these criteria nicely. It contains in a small area the major conflicts facing much of the Interior West. The arbitrarily defined boundary for this analysis then, is that area of land that has drainage into Running Creek — a region about 150 kilometers long and eight kilometers wide. Because natural, social, political, and economic elements of this system are to be considered, it is useful to think of it as a volume extending down to the coal beds and aquifers underlying the surface, and above ground far enough to incorporate problems of air pollution.

Having defined the system, a "systems approach" becomes, simply and perhaps circularly, a systematic analysis of this system. This analysis must specify some objective or objectives, and then assess the cost, effectiveness, and risk of various management strategies. This procedure, in turn, requires several steps, including: a) generating, compiling and synthesizing information about components of the system; b) examining the structure of the system; c) translating information about the systems structure into models useful for analysis and communication, and d) using these models to develop better understanding of the operation of the system and to evaluate management strategies that can be used to achieve the objectives specified. Models, as noted below, can range from simple verbal descriptions to complex mathematical simulations.

Participants at the Food, Fuel, and Shelter Conference focused on preliminary work on steps "a", "b", and "c". As noted above, some data gathering had already been done. Background papers written by members of the investigatory team provided additional data as well as examination of the structure of the system and its component parts. Conferees also relied on information provided by guest speakers, together with their own individual backgrounds and expertise. Working group discussions and plenary sessions included examination of the structure of the system and the building of a non-mathematical, descriptive model to identify trade-offs involved in the three development forms under consideration.

Modeling the Watershed

A model is simply an abstraction, or simplification, of a real system. Because even a narrowly defined system can be incredibly complex, all human thought involves the kind of simplifying abstraction provided by models. One does not, in contemplating a painting, consider the chemical composition of the paints, the physical properties that cause them to adhere to the canvas, or the nature of the light waves that provide for the perception of the painting's existence. One, instead, eliminates such considerations and focuses on a few that can be dealt with — perhaps form, color, and texture. Such a thought model is one kind of model of a system — in this case a painting — that is useful in its analysis. A written description of the painting would provide another model, one that would permit easy communication. It would even be possible to write a mathematical model specifying the location of various colors and textures and their relationships to one another. Such a model might prove useful in a comparative analysis of different works of art. And finally, the painting itself is a model of some other system — a bowl of fruit, the artist's perception of the nature of existence, or whatever.

In short, people deal with models of various kinds continuously; it is not surprising that models play a key role in the analysis of the watershed. The problem is to select the appropriate types of models for use in the inquiry. Verbal models, i.e. written or spoken descriptions and analyses of systems, are useful primarily because of their relative ease in communication to others. Such models are limited, however, in their ability to deal with complex relations among a wide range of factors. Visual models — charts, tables, maps, and graphs — retain the characteristic of ease of communication, while at the same time simplifying some complex relationships. These models are also limited in the number of relationships that can be dealt with simultaneously. Mathematical models, which typically require computers to speed up calculations, allow the analysis of quite complicated systems, but have a cost in terms of ease of communication. The greater the complexity, the greater the cost to others in understanding the structure of the model and its uses; care must be taken to make access by others to models as easy as possible. A further problem is the inclusion of social and humanistic elements which may be difficult to quantify.

The development of a mathematical model of the watershed system would have been far too complex a chore for a three-day conference. Preliminary exploration of the development of such a model is now underway at the Institute. Conferees focused on verbal and visual models designed to isolate and characterize trade-offs among land use alternatives. That work is discussed more fully in subsequent chapters; the general framework of the approach is presented here.

Trade-offs in Land Use

"Trade-off" is another term for cost — undertaking one activity at any time typically requires that another be given up at that time. The foregone activity represents a trade-off, or cost, of the activity chosen. Land cannot have houses or coal mines on it at the same time it is producing wheat; shelter or energy foregone can be regarded as the costs, or trade-offs, involved in agricultural production. Detailed analysis of these trade-offs requires a consideration of the possible shifts of land uses from one activity to another, together with the factors that affect these shifts.

Table 1.1 lists in the first vertical column major land use types that were considered at the conference. The remaining columns list these same land uses, this time as possible uses to which parcels in the first column might be converted. Checks indicate that such a conversion is a reasonable possibility over the twenty-five year period that conferees selected as a time horizon for the analysis. The checks in row 5, for example, represent a consensus that low density development (e.g. 10 acre ranchettes) is unlikely to be converted back to agricultural land, but that such land might be used for surface mining coal, and could also be converted to higher density uses. Conversion of low density development to agricultural uses is of course possible; it was simply considered unlikely that market or other forces would be sufficient to induce such a conversion in the face of the difficulties discussed in Chapter 4. Note, however that the conversions suggested in Table 1.1 remain reasonable possibilities — not forecasts of conversions for any one parcel of land.

Having identified possible land use changes, the next problem was to indicate factors that would influence rates at which these changes could be expected to occur. Table 1.1 suggests 28 different conversions of land use. These will be affected by environmental, economic, political, and social factors inside and outside the watershed. Table 1.2 gives a schema for classifying the roles of these factors. Each of the vertical columns of this matrix could be broken down still further; climate, for example, involves various aspects of temperature, precipitation, and wind. Each row in this matrix represents a land use change; checks in the column along a row will indicate that a factor influences the land use change.

Once the factors that affect land use changes are identified, the next step would be to specify the nature of these effects. A relatively flat topography, for example, is advantageous for crop production; it also makes for less expensive housing development, and may encourage such a conversion.

Another dimension of the problem that is of great importance is the impact of various shifts in land use on each other. For example, how does the change of land use of one parcel from pasture to medium density urban development affect the likelihood of a shift of adjoining parcels to medium density development, or to coal mining? These kinds of questions can be addressed by considering the effects of land use changes on factors which in turn influence the land use changes. Table 1.3 provides a format for this approach, which closes the circle of cause and effect. Land use changes are a response to factors inside and outside the system; these changes in turn affect factors within the system, influencing subsequent changes, and so on.

Out of this exercise of analysis grows increased understanding of the nature of the trade-offs involved, as well as an agenda for further research. The drastically simplified model of the watershed system suggested here has already become rather complicated — Tables 1.1 through 1.3 include 588 different relationships, most of which require further categorization for greater detail. Obviously, not all of these relationships were

Table 1.1 Land Use Conversion Matrix

			FOOD			FUEL	SHELTER		
			Irri-gation 1.	Dry-land 2.	Pas-ture 3.	Coal Strip 4.	Low Density 5.	Medium Density 6.	High Density 7.
FOOD	Irrigation	1.		X	X	X	X	X	X
	Dryland	2.	X		X	X	X	X	X
	Pasture	3.	X	X		X	X	X	X
FUEL	Coal Strip	4.	X	X	X		X	X	X
SHELTER	Low Density	5.				X		X	X
	Med. Density	6.							X
	High Density	7.							

A set of existing land uses is listed in the vertical column. Numbers on the top row correspond to these uses. The check in row 1, column 3 indicates that land now used in irrigated agriculture can be converted to pasture. The absence of checks in columns 1, 2 and 3 or rows 5, 6 and 7 suggests that a conversion from low, medium, or high density urban development to agriculture was viewed as unlikely.

specified in the short time available at the conference. But the experience of starting the task focused attention on research needs ahead.

The methodological approach described above provided a framework for the conference. Discussions at the meetings were lively; the work was intense. A regional focus on the issues raised in the Query workshop was achieved, and an agenda for future work developed. That future work, like the work of the conference itself, will be of great importance as people concerned about the region continue to grapple with difficult choices in the uses of scarce resources.

This report follows roughly the format of the conference itself. It examines the natural, economic, political, and social systems of the watershed, with particular emphasis on the response of these factors to land use changes, and the ways in which they may themselves induce such changes. Recent trends in urbanization and their effects on agriculture are given special emphasis. Prospective energy development and its likely effect on the watershed are discussed. Finally, the role of value systems and rights of future generations are considered.

Table 1.2 Factors Affecting Land Use Changes

	FACTORS									
	Environmental				Economic		Social-Political			
	Climate	Soils	Topography	Location	Demand	Supply Factors	Service Costs	Dominant Groups	Dominant Values	Jurisdictional Power
Irrigation to Dryland										
Irrigation to Pasture										
LAND USE CHANGES • • • • • • • • • • • • •										
Low Density to High Density										
Medium Density to High Density										

The vertical column lists the 28 land use changes identified in Table 1.1. Factors influencing the rate at which such changes are likely to occur are listed across the top. The work of identifying the nature of these effects is discussed below.

Table 1.3 Effects of Land Use Changes on Factors

	FACTORS	LAND USE CHANGES: Irrigation to Dryland	Irrigation to Pasture	• • • • • • • •	Low Density to High Density	Medium Density to High Density
ENVIRONMENTAL	Climate					
	Soils					
	Topography					
	Location					
ECONOMIC	Demand Factors					
	Supply Factors					
SOCIO-POLITICAL	Service Costs					
	Dominant Groups					
	Dominant Values					
	Jurisdictional Power					

The factors listed in Table 1.2 are listed here in the vertical column, with land use changes shifted to the top row. Effects identified here indicate that land use changes affect some of the factors that, in turn, will affect subsequent land use changes.

CHAPTER TWO

THE NATURAL SYSTEM

Soils and Topography: A Historical Sketch

Fences dominate the watershed landscape. They represent a system of property rights necessary to allocate land use functions; they also serve to keep cattle on their own range rather than trampling neighboring wheat fields. Because fences are familiar, they also serve as a useful model of geological time; Figure 2.1 uses the image of the barbed wire fence to trace more than a billion years of physical development of the Front Range Piedmont, of which the watershed is part.

Geological history is sobering, given the remarkably fleeting role man plays in it. The earliest evidence of man on the watershed is that of Folsom man, who hunted bison along Running Creek some 10,000 years ago. The human history of the watershed, spanning more than 10,000 years, takes up only ten sections of the fence in Figure 2.1.

A massive vertical uplift of land initiated the Tertiary period of the Cenozoic Era — some 65 to 50 million years ago. It started what was to become the modern Rocky Mountains. The lifting also affected the Great Plains, raising them from the sea and providing an eastward inclination. Subsequent erosion carried down gravel, sands, and clays from the fledgling Rockies, depositing these materials in a fan-like apron on the eastern shore. Much of the Front Range Piedmont is thus an alluvial plain; it is one of several places in the world in which such a plain has been formed at the base of a mountain range. These early run-off soils are the coarse, loosely cemented, sedimentary rocks of the Dawson Arkose formation. This formation, in which fossils of turtles and other vertebrates have been found, overlays the Laramie-Fox Hills sandstones. These porous rocks form an aquifer which in turn underlies much of the watershed. Water from the aquifer is used today for domestic as well as agricultural uses.

40 to 35 million years ago violent volcanic activity occurred in the region to the southwest and south. A fiery cloud of white-hot rhyolite ash burst from Wall Mountain near Salida in the mountains. It rushed across the country. In the vicinity of Castle Rock it settled into a thick layer still so hot that the particles fused into a solid mass. This is the Wall Mountain welded tuff. This fire-born rock soon fell to the disruptive forces of weathering. Fragments of it were rolled by running water and today are seen in the Castle Rock Conglomerate as pebbles from less than an inch to a yard across.

Erosion has played an important role in the development of the watershed. The South Platte and Arkansas River systems have carried away billions of tons of material swept from the mountains. The running water has channeled the alluvial apron of the mountains and excavated broad valleys lower than the plains that lie to the east. To the west of Running Creek are high hills capped with resistant welded tuff. These are slowly yielding to the forces of weathering and erosion.

Fig. 2.1 A Timeline History of Watershed and Related Events

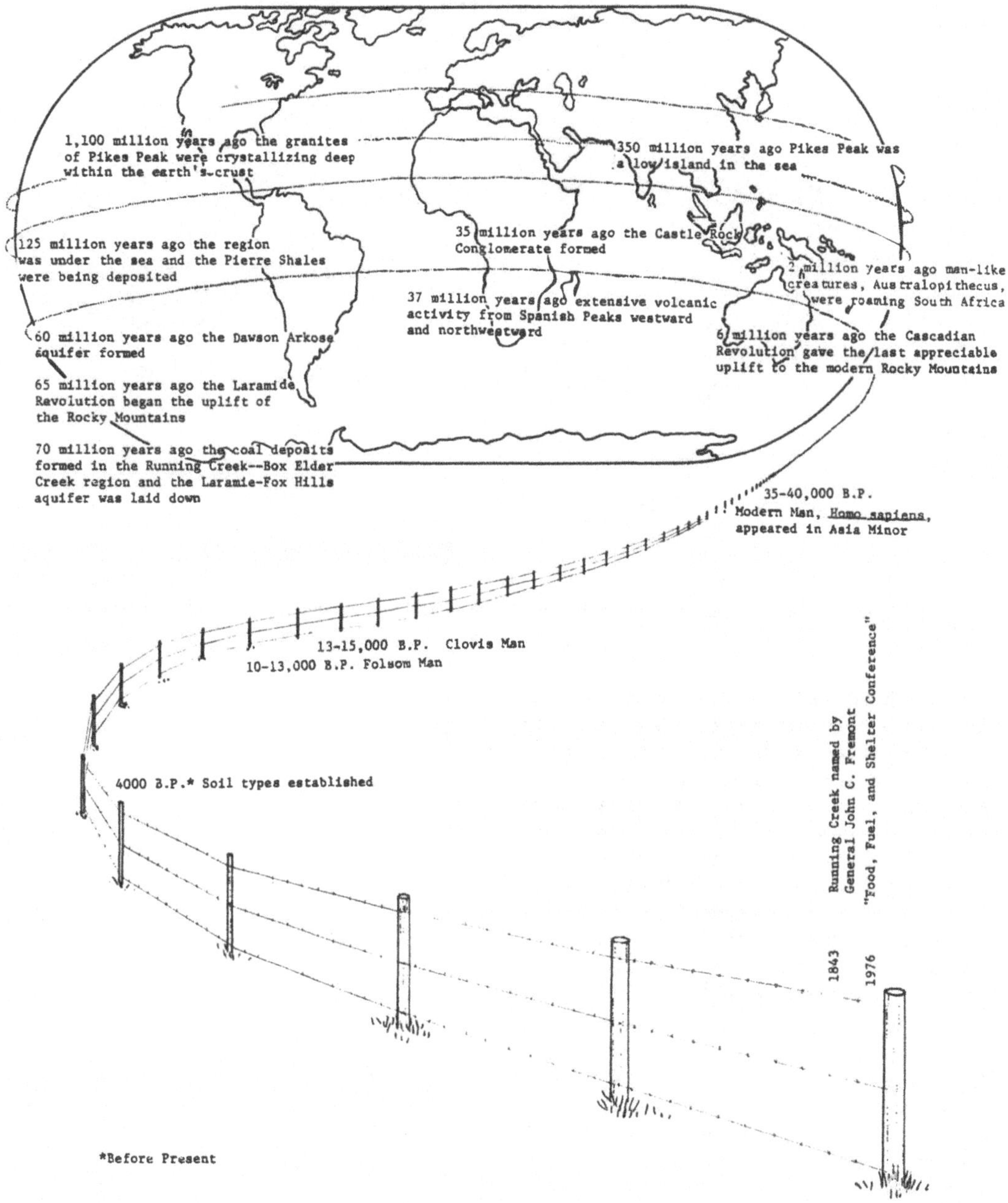

Picture of a barbed wire fence in 100-foot (30 m) sections; each 100' (30 m) section equal to 1,000 years of history. To illustrate the formation of the earth's resources and man-made history, the fence would start at Denver and run around the globe nearly 4 times to equal the age of the earth (5 billion years). (graphic by Doyle, 1977)

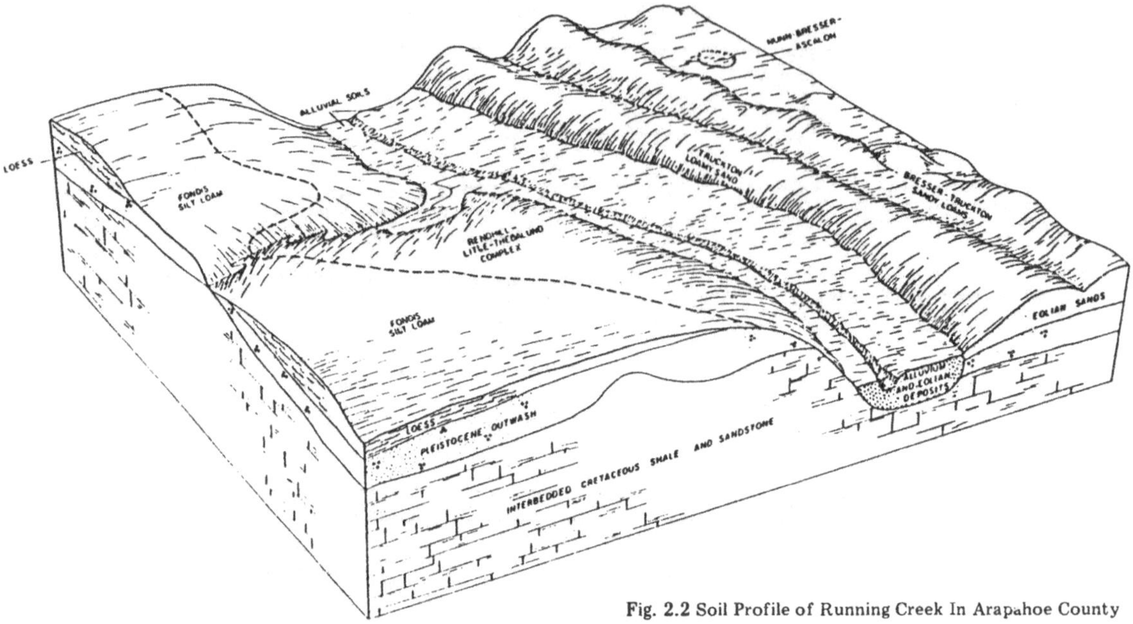

Fig. 2.2 Soil Profile of Running Creek In Arapahoe County

General landform features and underlying formation for Running Creek in Arapahoe County, Colorado (taken from Larsen and Brown 1971).

The materials that survived the erosion periods have thus changed little over time. The sandy soils at the headwaters of Running Creek are part of the Dawson Arkose formation. Further north near the center of the watershed in Arapahoe County, materials come from the Pierre Shale, Fox Hill, and Laramie formations of the upper Cretaceous age, as well as from the Dawson Arkose. Sands in this region are from the Recent age. These are added to annually as streams cut deeper into the rocks of the mountains. A soil profile for this area is sketched in Figure 2.2.

These watershed soils typically provide limited moisture storage. In Adams County, for example, less than eight centimeters of available moisture can be stored at any one time in soils with native grass cover. This moisture content is generally insufficient to provide for the displacement of salts in solution or colloids in suspension below a depth of about 30 centimeters in medium to moderately fine textured soils.

Climate*

The climate of the Front Range Piedmont is influenced by a number of large-scale features, or climatic controls. Smaller scale controls influence the watershed climate in particular, generating remarkable variations along its 150 kilometer length.

*This section based on George M. Van Dyne, "Renewable Resource Systems of the Running Creek (Box Elder) Area," paper prepared for the Food, Fuel, and Shelter Conference and Thomas McKee's conference presentation, "Climate Conditions Along the Front Range."

Large scale climatic controls that are important to the region include latitude, elevation, continentality, topography, and storm tracks. The latitude range of the watershed puts it in the line of predominant westerly wind currents, and accounts for its summer-winter seasonal patterns. Both these features are pronounced. Winds, which are strong in general on the Great Plains, are strongest from November to May on the watershed, with speeds in excess of 60 kilometers per hour common. Temperatures may exceed 40°C in the summer and drop below - 20° C in the winter.

The elevation of the watershed is important in its effect on temperature and moisture. Half of the water vapor in the earth's atmosphere is concentrated in the first 1800 meters above sea level; parts of the watershed are above that. The resultant drier air is a factor not only in the area's relative lack of rainfall — the climate is semi-arid — but in the pronounced diurnal changes in temperature. Daily temperature ranges often exceed 20°C on the watershed.

A primary factor responsible for the region's lack of moisture is its interior location in the North American continent on the east side of the Rocky Mountains. Pacific storms have generally lost their moisture by the time they pass over the Sierra Nevada and the Rocky Mountains. Most of the precipitation received in the watershed region

Table 2.1 Climatic Normals — Temperature (°C) (Twenty-year averages, 1951-1971)

	Elev (Meters)	Max	Min	ΔT	Max	Min	ΔT	>32.2	<-17.8
NORTH									
Greeley	1469	4.3	-13.4	17.7	32.7	13.7	19.0	18.0	8.0
Ft. Lupton	1545	5.3	-10.6	15.9	32.6	13.4	19.2	18.0	6.0
Longmont	1564	5.9	-11.4	17.3	31.4	12.8	18.6	15.0	6.0
CENTRAL									
Byers	1564	6.1	-10.1	16.2	32.4	13.6	18.8	18.0	5.0
Cherry Creek	1784	7.6	-9.3	16.9	31.4	12.8	18.6	16.0	4.0
Denver	1668	6.3	-8.9	15.2	30.8	14.4	16.4	16.0	4.0
SOUTH									
Castle Rock	1959	7.6	-11.0	18.6	30.2	11.5	18.7	18.7	6.0
Elbert	2130	6.5	-12.7	19.2	28.1	10.4	17.7	17.7	8.0
Parker	1950	6.3	-11.9	18.2	30.4	11.8	12.6	12.6	6.0

ΔT refers to the number of degrees difference between average minimum (Min) and average maximum (Max) temperatures; Max 32.2 figures are the number of days when the temperature exceeded 32.2°C; Min. -17.8 figures are the number of days when the temperature was below -17.8°C.

Table 2.2 Climatic Normals — Precipitation (Twenty-year averages, 1951-1971)

	Period	Annual (cm)	Snow (cm)	1.25 Centimeters	2.5 Centimeters
NORTH					
Greeley	37	28.5	75	6.6	1.3
Ft. Lupton	40	31.3	83	6.7	1.6
Longmont	42	30.8	90	6.2	1.8
CENTRAL					
Byers	42	36.8	113	8.2	2.6
Cherry Creek	22	29.3	148	8.2	2.7
Denver	25	38.0	158	7.7	2.2
SOUTH					
Castle Rock	15	39.5	158	7.7	2.6
Elbert	10	40.3	138	8.0	2.5
Parker	42	33.3	138	8.1	2.0

Period indicates the number of days when precipitation occurred.
Annual (cm) and Snow (cm) refer to the amounts of precipitation and snow measured in centimeters.
Figures in the 1.25 Centimeters and 2.5 Centimeters columns refer to the number of days when the precipitation was greater than 1.25 cm and greater than 2.5 cm in one day, respectively.

Fig. 2.3 Temperature and Precipitation Recording Stations

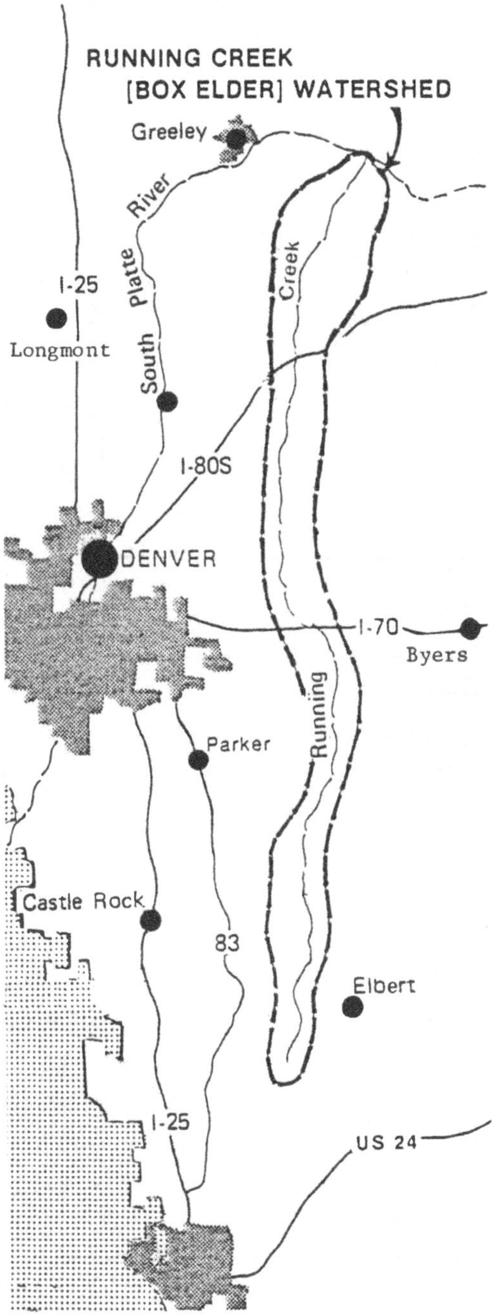

Location of temperature and precipitation recording stations with data included in this report. These stations are maintained by the US Weather Bureau.

must travel up from the Gulf of Mexico. The storm tracks in the watershed region are quite variable; this may be a factor in producing climatic changes over time.

Localized controls important in inducing variations in climate within the watershed include land form, orientation and location, elevation, slope and aspect, surface soils, vegetation, and human development. The north-south orientation of the watershed influences the course of storm tracks. The north end of the watershed is a localized low spot, one that is frequently missed by summer and winter storms. Its annual precipitation of about 30 centimeters makes it one of the driest spots in Colorado. Moving south, up the watershed, annual precipitation increases to about 37 centimeters in the central region, and averages about 42 centimeters annually at the southern end. A perhaps more striking contrast is snowfall measured at two points near the watershed. Greeley, in the low area at the northern end, averages 75 centimeters snowfall per year. Denver, about 35 kilometers west of the middle region of the watershed, averages 158 centimeters.

Temperature and precipitation data are given in Tables 2.1 and 2.2 for nine measuring stations located near the northern, central, and southern regions of the watershed. Figure 2.3 shows the location of these stations, together with other stations cited below in the analysis. Figure 2.4 gives mean annual temperatures for Greeley, Byers, Parker, and Elbert. There is no apparent long term trend in either precipitation or temperature for any of these sites; note the lack of trend in Figure 2.4 and in Figure 2.5, which gives Greeley precipitation. Computing lengths of the growing season for towns cited in Figure 2.6 (a growing season is defined as a period in which the temperature does not fall below 0°C); however, reveals a slight downward trend, as shown in Figure 2.6.

Fig. 2.4 Time Series of Mean Annual Temperatures

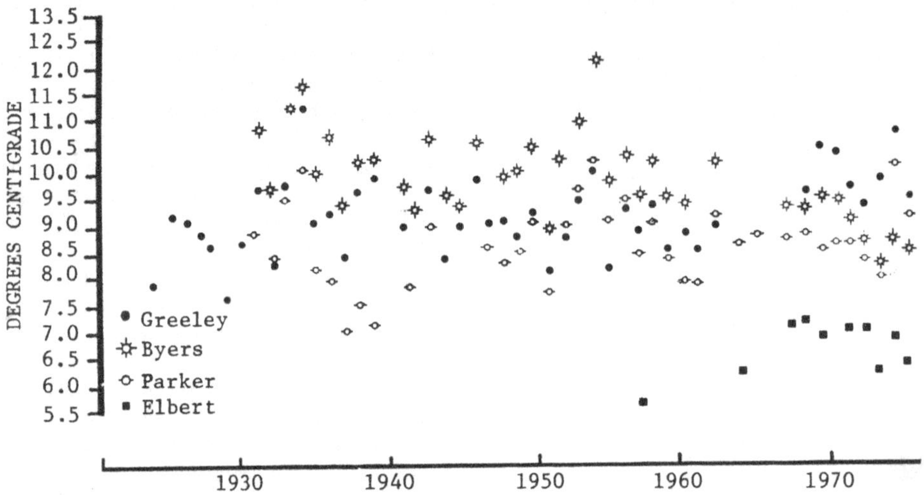

Fig. 2.5 Time Series of Greeley Precipitation

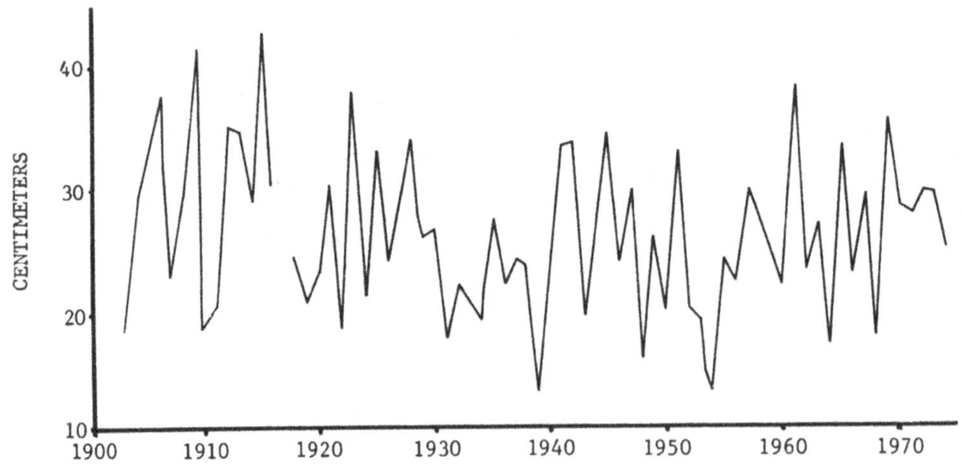

Fig. 2.6 Time Series of Lengths of Growing Seasons.

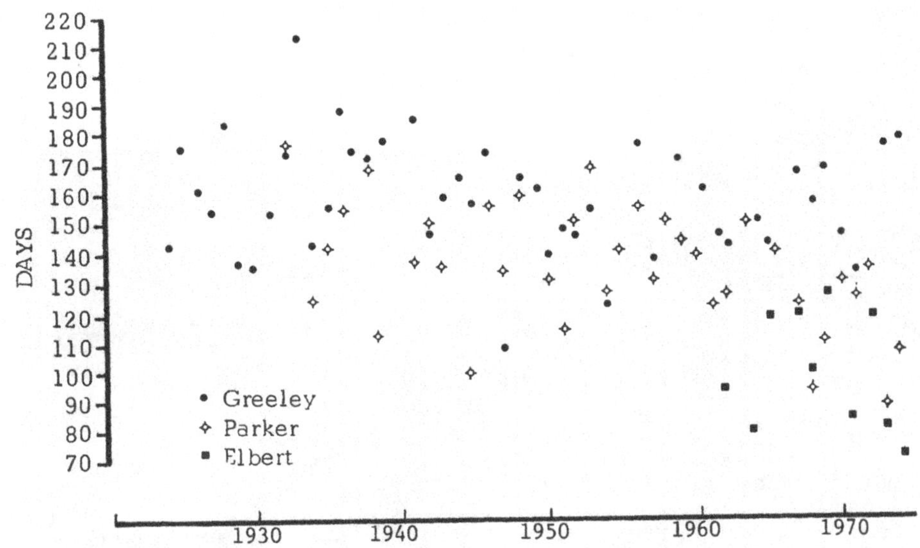

See Fig. 2.3 for locations of stations

Fig. 2.7 Precipitation by Month

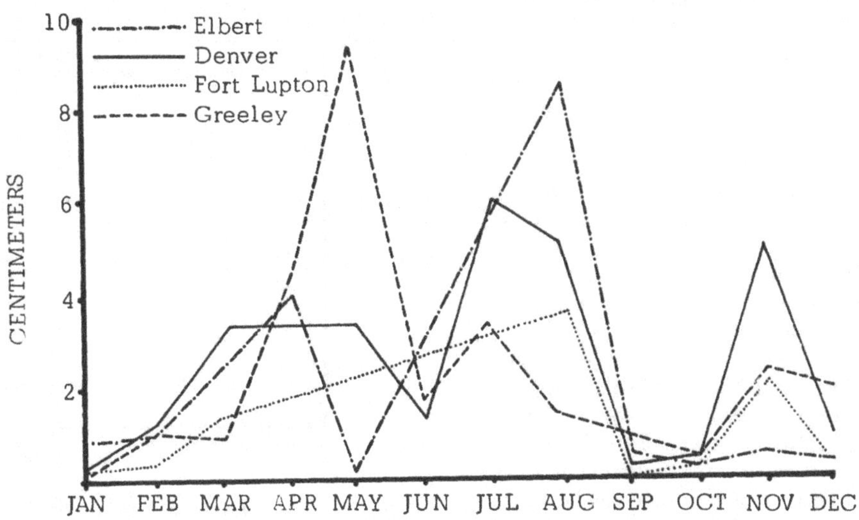

Data drawn from 1975 US Dept. of Commerce, Climatological Data

Approximately three-fourths of the region's annual precipitation occurs from April to November, as suggested in Figure 2.7. This creates a difficulty. These summer season storms are typically of high density and short duration. They thus tend to be characterized more by rapid run-off and soil erosion than by useful additions to soil moisture. Figure 2.8 illustrates this point well. Percentage of annual precipitation is plotted on the vertical axis; percentage of days on which precipitation occurred is on the horizontal. Precipitation by day for Denver was tabulated for the period 1948-1972, with the days ordered from highest to lowest in precipitation. If each day with precipitation had had an equal amount of precipitation, then there would be a 45° line relationship between the two variables plotted, e.g. 20 percent of the days would have accounted for 20 percent of the percipitation. But precipitation is obviously greater on some rainy or snowy days than on others; the degree of inequality is shown by the degree to which the actual curve is bowed out from the 45° line. In the case of Denver, 40 percent of the days with precipitation accounted for

Fig. 2.8 Denver Precipitation: 1948-1972

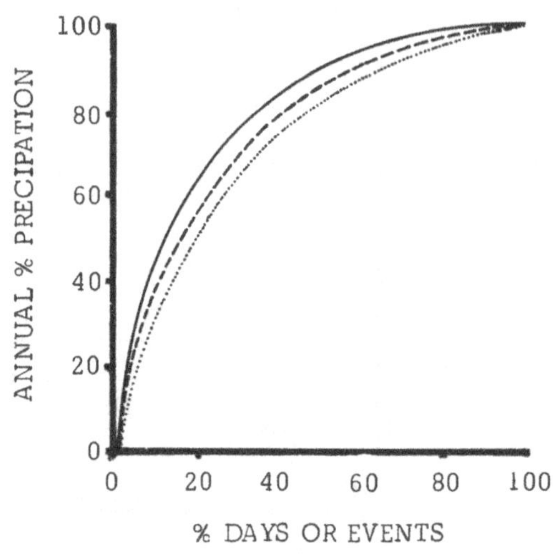

Fig. 2.9 Time Series of Precipitation

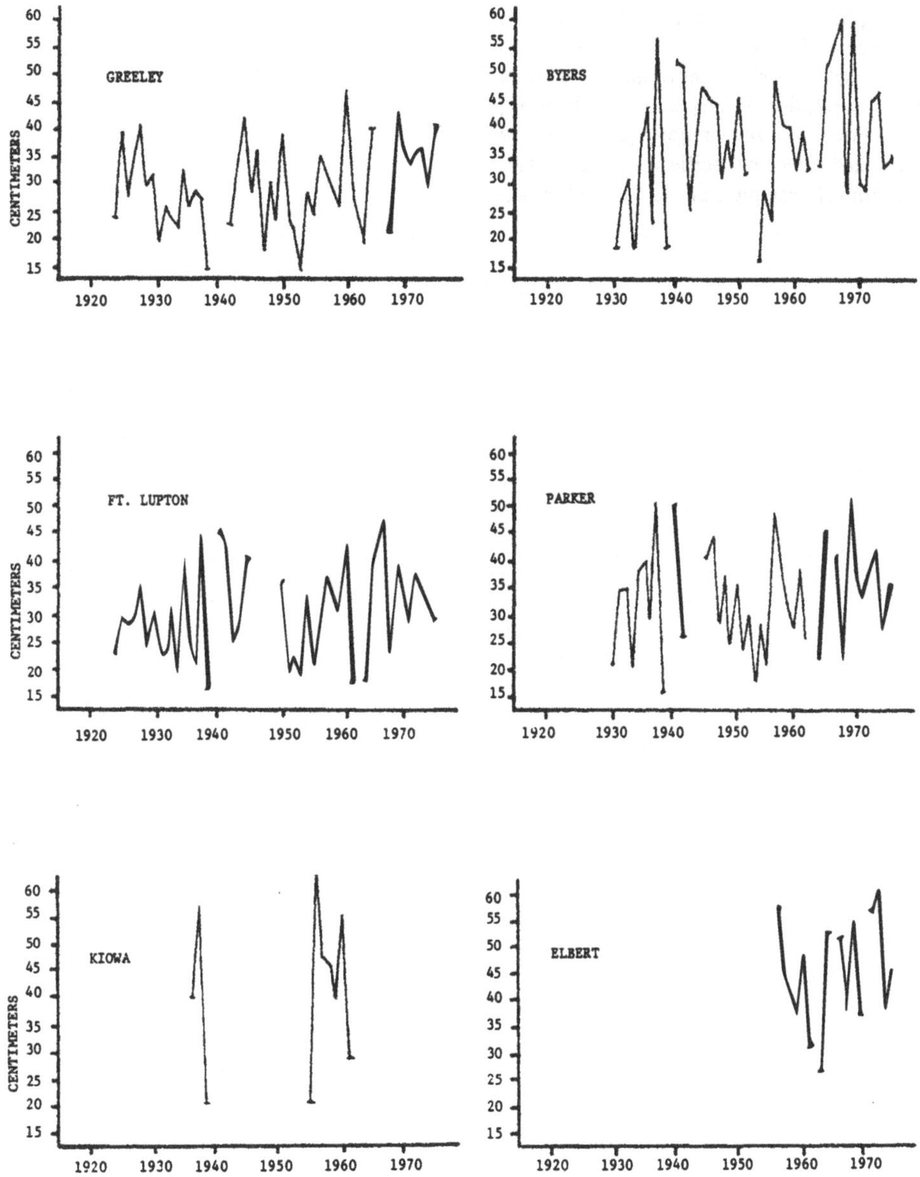

Precipitation data for major towns in or near the Running Creek watershed in the last 50 years. For locations see Fig. 2.3

more than 80 percent of total precipitation. The dotted line component of the figure shows the snow-fall component of precipitation; it shows a more even distribution.

Most rainy days in the watershed thus do not contribute much; it is the relatively small number of big precipitation events that provide for most of the moisture. The timing of these events thus becomes crucial — perhaps more important than the total precipitation in any one year. Further, the importance of a few major events that are highly localized subjects specific sites to great variability in annual precipitation, as Figure 2.9 suggests.

Native Vegetation*

The native vegetation of a region depends upon, and in turn influences, climate and soil conditions. It plays, as noted in Chapter Three, a crucial role in the agricultural base of the watershed economy. Four general vegetation types cover the watershed: Montane forest, oakbrush-chaparral, grasslands, and sandhill. These regions are mapped in Figure 2.10; note the predominance of grasslands in the region.

Montane Forest

The montane forest region of the watershed is part of the Black Forest of Colorado. The forest is located at the divide separating the South Platte and Arkansas river systems. The summit of this divide is at an elevation of 2250 meters; some areas of the forest are found at elevations as low as 1800 meters. The forest contains substantial stands of Ponderosa pine, with some Douglas fir, aspen, and junipers. Much of it played an important role in the settling of the watershed by pioneers; it was cut down for lumber in the latter part of the 19th century. Logging operations aside, the chief factor in the location of the forest is soil moisture. Soils in the forest area are coarse in texture, resulting in rapid infiltration of precipitation and reduced run-off. This permits the accumulation and storage of water down to the underlying conglomerate rock, providing trees with reserves of moisture at considerable depths.

Grasslands species in the montane forest include prairie dropseed, needlegrass, and Kentucky bluegrass at higher elevations. Lower elevation forest sites are dominated by prairie dropseed alone.

Oakbrush-Chaparral

Soils similar to those of the montane forest, but at lower elevations with less precipitation and higher temperatures, sustain the oakbrush-chaparral community. This vegetation includes scrub oak, mountain mahogany, and wild rose. The oakbrush-chaparral community is widely interspersed with grassland species including blue grama, mountain muhly, needle-and-thread, and prairie sandreed.

Grasslands

Grasslands dominate the watershed, marking it as part of a transition area moving from the Rocky Mountains to the Great Plains. Four major vegetation types cover the Great Plains, as well as the grasslands area of the watershed. These are shortgrass prairie, wiregrass, bunchgrass, and sandhills mixed prairie.

Montane Forest

*This section based on George M. Van Dyne, "Renewable Resource Systems of the Running Creek (Box Elder) Area."

Fig. 2.10 Natural Vegetation of the Watershed

GRASSLANDS

Blue grama
Sand dropseed
Three-awn
Prairie Sand reed
Sand blue stem
Sideoats grama
Yucca

GRASSLANDS

Sand reed
Sand blue stem
Sand dropseed
Sand sage

GRASSLANDS

Blue grama
Buffalo grass
Alkali sakaton
Sand dropseed
Inland saltgrass
Sedges
Four-wing saltbrush
Winterfat

GRASSLANDS (Foothills)

Mountain muhly
Wheatgrass
Needle-and-thread
Blue stem
Blue grama
Six-weeks fescue
Scrub Oak
Mountain mahogany
Thimbleberry
Wax Current
Wild rose

FOREST

Ponderosa Pine
Junipers

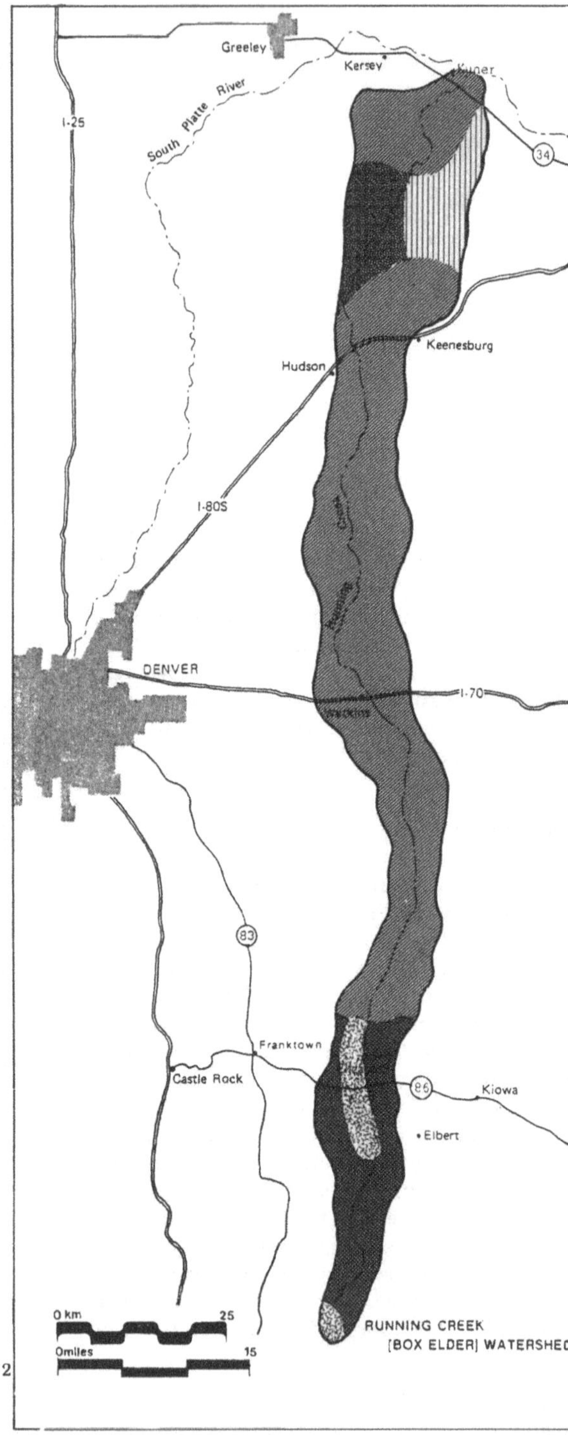

from: USDA-SCS "Natural Vegetation of Colorado", 1972

Blue grama grass
Bouteloua gracilis

(from USDA, *Manual of Grasses of the United States*, A.S. Hitchcock, 1950)

Shortgrass Prairie

Blue grama and buffalograss are the most important species on the shortgrass prairie, a region in which available moisture is typically confined to the first 60 centimeters of soil. Both of these grasses survive desiccation and are quick to revive when water is again available. But perhaps the most important factor is the phenology of the two grasses. Both require only a short time to mature. Buffalograss and Blue grama are typically warm season grasses which are not available for grazing in early April. The combination of these warm season grasses with the cool season grasses provides a long period of green feed for grazing. In general, some 10 to 15 per cent of the biomass generated in the shortgrass prairie is comprised of cool season species; the remainder is made up of warm season species.

Depending on moisture, blue grama can bloom from late May to late June and again in August. It is unusual in this respect. Generally, species that reach peak bloom before early June or after August flower only once, while those blooming between these periods may bloom more often.

Buffalograss is more common in soils that are heavy in texture than in light-textured soils. Common secondary grasses and sedges in these heavier soils of the shortgrass prairie include western wheatgrass, needle-and-thread, alkali sakaton, sand dropseed, inland saltgrass, and threadleaf and needleleaf sedges. Three-awn grasses (wiregrass) are common in soil that has been disturbed. Perennial forbs in these sites include scurfpea, scarlet globemallow, and slenderbrush eriogonum. Two shrubs in these communities, four-wing saltbrush and winterfat, provide good forage for cattle. Other shrubs, such as rubber rabbitbrush, broom snakeweed, and fringed sagewort, are relatively unpalatable.

Wiregrass

The second grasslands vegetation type, wiregrass, occurs on sandy loam soils characterized by substantial penetration of rainfall. These areas have shortgrasses such as blue grama and hairy grama, as well as taller plants such as red three-awn and scurfpea. Other common plants include needle-and-thread, sand dropseed, needleleaf sedge, tumblegrass, and six-weeks fescue. Conditions in wiregrass communities are favorable for both shallow and deep-rooted plants for a longer period of time than those in the shortgrass prairie.

Sandhills

The sandhills vegetation type occurs in widely varying topographical conditions and has a diverse botanical composition. It is characterized primarily by the prevalence of prairie sandreed, rice grass, and sand bluestem. Sand sagebrush is another plant characteristic of this type. Forbs include bush morning glory and small soapweed. Sandhills areas are more subject to blowing sands than are the other grassland types; "blow-outs" are common in plowed areas. The least resistant to drought of the grasslands areas, sandhills are the most productive of the four in years of high precipitation.

Bunchgrass

Rainfall deeply penetrates sandy soils where there is little run-off or evaporation. These conditions support the bunchgrass vegetation type. Little bluestem, a midgrass in eastern Colorado, forms a fairly dense cover in these areas. It is the reddish brown plant noticeable particularly in the fall and winter. Other important grasses of the bunchgrass vegetation type include sand bluestem, prairie sandreed grass, switchgrass, red three-awn, blue grama, and hairy grama. Plants of the bunchgrass areas provide the greatest production of the four grassland types during extremely dry years.

George M. Van Dyne

Animal Life

The watershed has a rich variety of wildlife. Common mammals in the area include antelope, mule deer, white-tail deer, white-tail jackrabbits, black-tail jackrabbits, 13-line ground squirrels, northern grasshopper mice, kangaroo rats, and deer mice. Other small rodents, such as chipmunks, marmots, prairie dogs, squirrels, other mice, voles, packrats, and porcupines are also found. Important carnivores include coyotes, foxes, raccoons, ermines, weasels, ferrets, badgers, and bobcats.

At least 15 species of reptiles can be found in shortgrass prairie regions of the watershed, including lizards, snakes, and turtles. Amphibians include the spadefoot toad, numerous frogs, and salamanders.

Prairie birds include the lark bunting and horned lark. Waterways are frequented by plovers, curlews, sandpipers, gulls, killdeers, mallards, gadwalls, pintails, and teals. Birds that can be found throughout the watershed include kingbirds, flycatchers, swallows, jays, magpies, crows, chickadees, nuthatches, wrens, thrashers, shrikes, warblers, thrushes, meadowlarks, blackbirds, orioles, finches, towhees, sparrows, juncos, and longspurs. Raptorial birds may play a more important role in grasslands than in other ecosystems, consuming nearly every species of bird, mammal, and reptile found on the prairie. Watershed raptorial birds include hawks, eagles, and owls.

Thousands of insect species exist in the watershed. Scarab beetles are quite common in the soil. There are more than 30 types of grasshoppers in the watershed.

Figure 2.11 gives a census of wildlife on the shortgrass prairie. Measurements of grams per hectare (wet weight) at the Pawnee site north of the watershed found the following averages for areas under a range of grazing intensities: all consumers, 16,446; cattle, 15,700; invertebrates, 630; small mammals, 96; and nesting birds, 20. Consumer biomass varies positively with the abundance of plant life, or net primary productivity, as shown in Figure 2.12. Note that the relationship is an exponential one. Grasslands with midgrasses should have 50-100 percent more consumer biomass than those with shortgrasses. Areas with tall grasses can be expected to have five times the consumer biomass of that found on the shortgrass prairie.

Cattle are the dominant species on the watershed by weight; blue grama grass is, in turn, the most important part of the cattle diet by weight. Table 2.3 gives the percentages of blue grama in the diets of important herbivores on the watershed.

Table 2.3 Blue Grama Percentage in Diets of Watershed Herbivores

Animal	Percentage
Buffalo	58
Cattle	44
Sheep	34
Antelope	10
Jackrabbit	7

Prairie dog

Fig. 2.11 Estimates of numbers (per hectare) of various mammal, insect, and bird species on the shortgrass prairie.

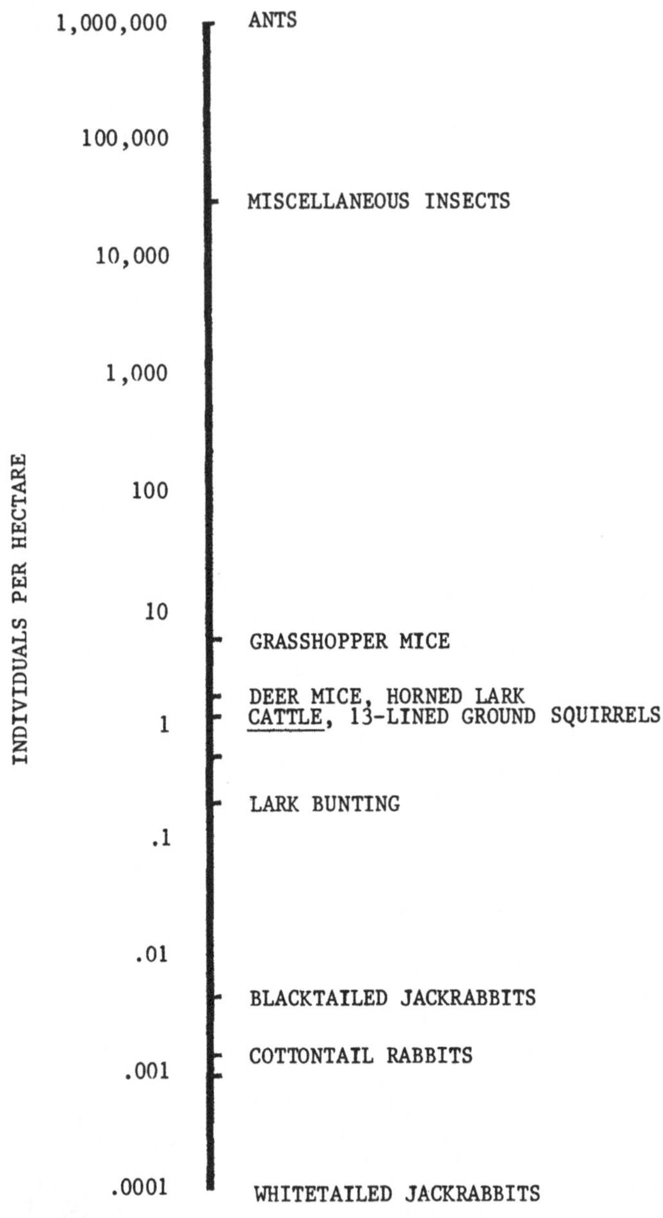

Fig. 2.12 Animal Biomass and Plant Production in Arid and Semi-Arid Western North American Grasslands

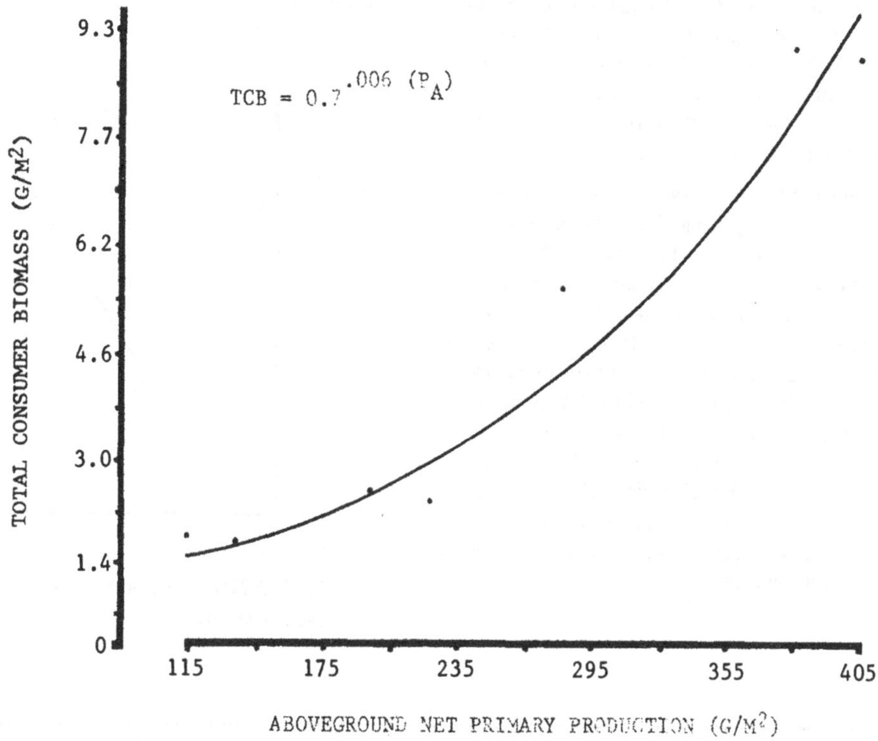

Relationship between production by plants and animal biomass in arid and semiarid western North American Grasslands. (Van Dyne 1971)

Table 2.4 Dietary Preference Values for Large Herbivores for Summer Grazing on a Shortgrass Prairie

Item	Cattle	Bison	Sheep	Antelope
Warm-season grasses	34	30	6	2
Cool-season grasses	16	27	4	1
Forbs	49	43	89	96
Shrubs	1	1	1	1

Numbers listed are derived by dividing the percentage of each vegetation type in the diet of each animal (by weight) by the percentage of that vegetation type of total herbage available.

Dietary preference ratios have been calculated for cattle, buffalo, sheep, and antelope on the shortgrass prairie. The numbers in Table 2.4 give the ratio of the percentage of each vegetation type by weight in the diet of each animal to the percentage of that vegetation type to total herbage available. Note the preference for forbs by all species, particularly sheep and antelope. Cattle and sheep, the introduced herbivores, are more alike than the native buffalo and antelope.

Birds rely heavily on insects in their diet. It is therefore perhaps surprising that there is no close relationship between insect biomass and bird biomass in any one year. There is, however, a strong lagged relationship between these two variables; bird biomass in any one year depends on insect biomass in the previous year, as shown in Figure 2.13. The main influence of the insect population on birds thus appears to operate through rates of fledgling success and return. Table 2.5 gives percentages of summer diet of birds in the consumption of seeds and invertebrates. Table 2.6 gives the consumption categories of common invertebrates on the watershed.

Fig. 2.13 Relationship between insect abundance one year and bird abundance the next year on several western North American grasslands.

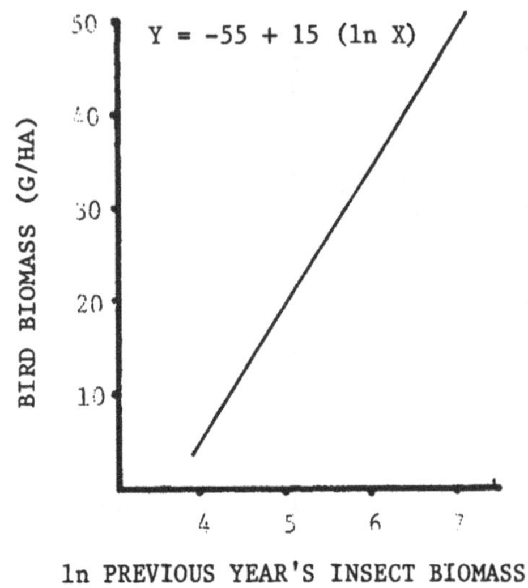

(Van Dyne 1971)

Table 2.5 Seeds and Invertebrates in the Summer Diets of Grasslands Birds
Food habits of common grassland birds from the Running Creek watershed are summarized as follows:
(Van Dyne 1971)

SPECIES	Percent of Summer Diet	
	Seeds	Invertebrates
Horned lark	80	20
Grasshopper Sparrow	35	65
Dickcissel	30	70
Chestnut-colored longspur	50	50
Lark bunting	40	60
Meadow lark	0	100
Upland plover	0	100
Long-billed curlew	0	100

Table 2.6 General food habit characteristics for some important invertebrates on shortgrass prairie in northeastern Colorado (Van Dyne 1971)

Order or Class	Family	Common Name	Herbivores	Carnivores	Scavengers	Microflora	Microfauna
Acarina						●	●
Araneida							
	Lycosidae	Wolf spiders		●			
	Salticidae	Jumping spiders		●			
Chilopoda		Centipedes		●			
Diplopoda		Millipedes			●		
Coleoptera		Beetles					
	Anthicidae	Antlike flower beetles	●				
	Anthribidae	Fungus weevils				●	
	Bruchidae	Seed beetles	●				
	Carabidae	Ground beetles		●			
	Cerambycidae	Long-horned wood boring beetles	●				
	Chrysomelidae	Leaf beetles	●				
	Coccinellidae	Ladybird beetles		●			
	Curculionidae	Snout beetles	●				
	Elateridae	Click beetles	●				
	Lathridiidae	Minute brown scavenger beetles				●	
	Malachiidae	Soft-winged flower beetles		●			
	Meloidae	Blister beetles		●			
	Nitidulidae	Sap-feeding beetles	●	●	●	●	●
	Phalacridae	Shining flower beetles					●
	Pselaphidae	Ant-loving beetles					
	Scaphidiidae	Carrion or burying beetles					●
	Scarabaeidae	Scarab bettles			●		
	Staphylinidae	Rove beetles			●		
	Tenebrionidae	Darkling beetles			●		
Collembola		Springtails					
	Entomobryidae	Elongate-boiled springtails			●		
	Sminthuridae	Globular springtails	●		●		
Diptera		Flies					
	Agromzidae	Leaf-miner flies	●				
	Anthomyiidae	Anthomylid flies					
	Asilidae	Robber flies		●			
	Cecidomyiidae	Gall gnats	●				
Diptera (cont.)	Ceratopogonidae						
	Chironomidae						
	Chloropidae						
	Muscidae						
	Mycetophilidae						
	Phoridae						
	Sarcophagidae						
	Simulidae						
	Tachinidae						
Hemiptera	Coreidae						
	Lygaeidae						
	Miridae						
	Nabidae						
	Pentatomidae						
	Phymatidae						
	Plesidae						
	Reduviidae						
	Scutelleridae						
	Tingidae						
Homonoptera	Aphididae						
	Cercopidae						
	Cicadellidae						
	Coccidae						
	Dactylopiidae						
	Fulgoridae						
Hymonoptera	Andrenidae						
	Braconidae						
	Chalcedectidae						
	Chalcididae						
	Dryinidae						
	Encyrtidae						
	Eulophidae						
	Eurytomidae						
	Formicidae						

Common Name	Herbivores	Carnivores	Scavengers	Microflora	Microfauna
Punkles		●			
Midges					
Frit flies	●				
Muscid flies			●		
Fungus gnats					
Humpbacked flies					
Flesh flies		●			
Black flies		●			
Tachinid flies		●			
Bugs					
Leaf-rooted bugs	●				
Lygaeid bugs					
Leaf or plant bugs					
Damsel bugs	●				
Stink bugs	●				
Ambush bugs		●			
Ash-gray leaf bugs	●				
Assasin bugs					
Shield-backed bugs	●				
Lace bugs					
Aphids or plant lice	●				
Froghoppers or sprittle bugs	●				
Leafhoppers	●				
Scale insects and mealy bugs	●				
Cochineal insects	●				
Fulgorid plant hoppers	●				
Andrenid bees		●			
Braconids					
Chalcedectids					
Chalcidids	●	●			
Dryinids		●			
Encyrtids		●			
Eulophids		●			
Eurytomids or seed chalcids	●				
Ants	●	●			

Order or Class	Family	Common Name	Herbivores	Carnivores	Scavengers	Microflora
Hymonoptera (cont.)	Ichneumonides	Ichneumons		●		
	Pteromalidae	Pteromalids				
	Tiphiidae	Tiphids		●		
	Thysanidae	Thysanids		●		
	Trichogrammatids	Trichogrammatids		●		
Leidoptera	Arctiidae	Tiger moths	●			
	Gelechiidae	Gelechid moths	●			
	Nocturidae	Noctuid moths	●			
	Pyralidae	Pyralid moths	●			
	Tineidae	Clothes moths	●			
	Tortricidae	Tortricids	●			
Neuoptera	Hemerobiidae	Brown lacewings		●		
	Myremeliontidae	Ant lions		●		
Orthoptera	Acrididae	Short-horned grasshoppers	●			
	Mantidae	Mantids		●		
	Phasmidae	Walkingsticks				
	Tettigonidae	Long-horned grasshoppers	●			
Psocoptera	Book lice and bark lice					
	Liposcelidae	Liposcelid book lice	●		●	●
Thysanura	Lepismatidae	Silverfish				
	Machilidae	Jumping bristletails	●			●
Thysanoptera	Phloeothripidae	Tube-tailed thrips	●			
	Thripidae	Thrips	●			

Table 2.7 A "who eats whom or what" matrix for various consumers on the shortgrass plains of the Pawnee National Grassland of northeastern Colorado. The 32 consumer groups listed in the vertical column are important consumers in the community. Food items are listed along the top row. (Harris, L.D., L. Paur, A Quantitative Food Web Analysis of a Shortgrass Community, Grasslands Biome Study, Tech. Rep. 154, 1972.).

	Ironplant goldenweed Three-cleft greenthread Cryptantha species Cheat grass brome Rodowski's stickweed	Groundsel-senecio species Dandelion Woolly Indian Wheat Prairie pepperweed Groundsel-Senecio multicapitatus	Fringed sagewort Blue grama Belvedere summer cypress Scarlet globemallow cutleaf evening primrose	Slimflower scurfpea Needle and thread Hairy golden aster Red three-awn Locoweed	Carex Sand dropseed Western wheatgrass Gromwell Broom snakeweed	Six-weeks fescue Wavyleaf thistle Buffalo grass Crested wheatgrass Alfalfa	Tumbling Russian thistle Four-o-clock Silky sophora Unknown vegetation Wheat	Oats Common sunflower Unknown forbs Rubber rabbit brush Bee spiderflower
ANTELOPE	10 9 4 1 1	1 1 5 3 6	8 10 2 26					
CATTLE			1 44 1 5 2	5 10 1 3 1	14 1 7 1			
SHEEP			1 34 26 2	1 3	18 1 4 5	11		
BISON			58 .86	.03 .04	5 3 18	1 1 4		
BLACK-TAILED JACKRABBIT		1	8 21 1	5	3 6 9	4 6 8	1 2 2 1 4	2 1
WHITE-TAILED JACKRABBIT		1	8 11 2 2	10	7 2 29	11 1 1	1 2 2 1 9	1
GRASSHOPPER-Opeia obscura			96		1 3			
GRASSHOPPER-Trachrachys kiowa			97		3			
GRASSHOPPER-Psolessa delicatula			98		2			
GRASSHOPPER-Arphia pseudonietana			90		26 4			14
GRASSHOPPER-Melanoplus infantilis					42 54			7 2
COLEOPTERA			4 5 1	12 4 1 5	1 25	10		2 5
DIPTERA			5		36	10	2 1	2 1
HEMIPTERA			8 8	4 2 1	1 2 30	9		
GOPHER			10 3 27	2 2 2	3 13		8	
KANGAROO RAT			6 8		1	3	2	
HARVESTER ANT		12		1 1 9		1 3	3 4	
HORNED LARK			1				2	3
LARK BUNTING					5		5	2 3
McCOWN'S LONGSPUR					1	6	2	1
CHESTNUT-COLLARED LONGSPUR								
ROBBER FLY							1	1 4
GROUND SQUIRREL		2 1	9 1 3	1	1 1	1		
DEER MOUSE			1 6 3					
GRASSHOPPER MOUSE			5 1 3		1			
GREAT HORNED OWL								
BURROWING OWL								
LONG-EARED OWL								
BARN OWL								
GOLDEN EAGLE								
FERRUGINOUS HAWK								
SWAINSON'S HAWK								

Dotted gayfeather Pinnate tansy mustard Fourwing saltbrush Bottlebrush squirreltail Plains bahia	Plains prickly pear Greenthread Groundsel, Senecio tridenticulatus Small soapweed Upright prairie coneflower	Prairie spiderwort Unidentified seeds Fungus Common buckwheat Tansyleaf aster	Lambsquarter Cream peavine Slenderbrush buckwheat Cryptantha minima orchard grass	Canada wild rye Wild rye Wild buckwheat Peavine Silky crazyweed	Musincon Bush peavine Knotweed Indian ricegrass Fendler three awn	Tumbleweed amaranth Slimleaf goosefoot Lichen Unidentified grasshopper Ants	Butterflies Lace wings Beetles Spiders Miscellaneous	Flies, mosquitoes True bugs Burrowing owl Leafhoppers, aphids, etc. Dragonflies	Crickets Housemouse Cottontail rabbit Prairie vole Horned lark
1 2 4 1 1 2 7 11 2 6 1 7	1 5 12 1 2 24	1 64 3							
			5 3 7 11	1 1 1 11	1 1 1 6 5 7 8 1 13 46	2 1 72 4 19 11 18 12 17	1 10 2 1 29 1 1 29 2 2 25	2 1 1 2 2 1 3 4 3	
1 1	1	1 12 8 23 3 3 1			1 1	26 12 1 7 3 1 4 1 17 1	5 2 4 6 26 1 9 14 2 3 3 55 3 1	35 3 13 1 1 1	86
						1	3 2	7 2	3 1 42 13 67 14 20 27 24 1 11 4

Fig. 2.14 Some main food chain relationships among some major components of the natural grasslands of the Running Creek watershed

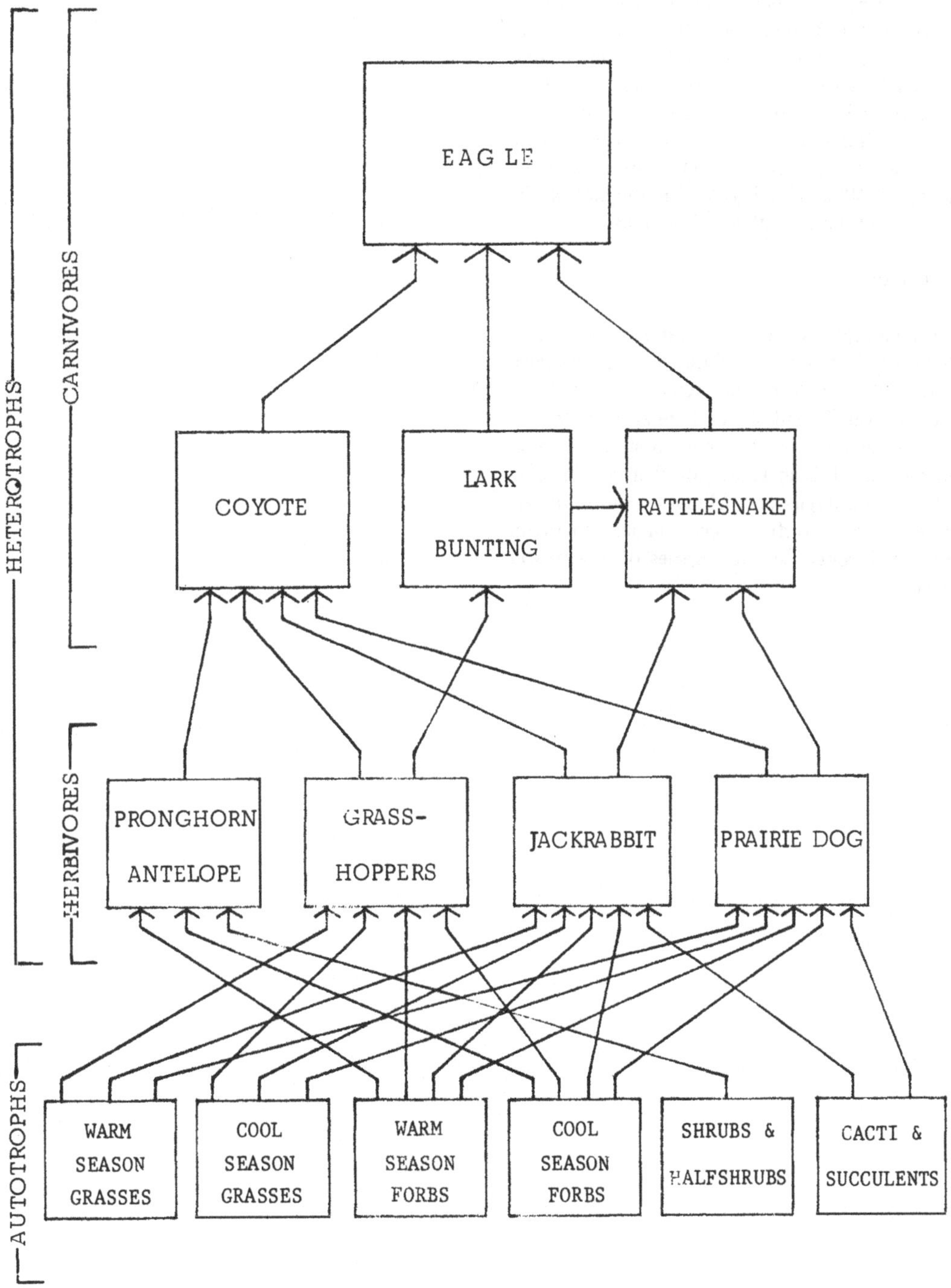

The entire food chain of the watershed is quite complex. An analysis of this chain at a site north of the watershed is presented in Table 2.7. This table presents information on the diets of 32 consumers and 112 food items. The consumers are listed in individual rows in the "*who eats whom, or what*" matrix. Consumption items — which include several of the consumers — are listed by columns. Numerical entries in the cells indicate percentage weights in the diet. Note that of the more than 4000 possible entries in the matrix, the food chain follows relatively few paths.

Conclusion

The natural system of the watershed is a complex one; what is known about it seems insignificant, relative to work that remains to be done. But even the limited sketch here suggests the remarkable adaptation of species to an often harsh environment. It is an adaptation that may in some respects be a fragile one. Climatic changes in particular have powerful effects on an ecosystem carefully adapted to the vagaries of a semi-arid climate.

CHAPTER THREE

AGRICULTURE: THE ECONOMIC BASE OF THE WATERSHED

Introduction

The discussion in Chapter Two of the "natural system" suggests that perhaps it should be followed by an examination of the unnatural one. But the economic system of any region can hardly be described as unnatural; indeed, the watershed economic system depends heavily on the "natural" forces discussed in Chapter Two, and many of the economic principles under which it operates are analagous to those of the natural system.

Foundations: The Economic Base*

Economic activity is fundamentally a process of exchange. Individuals are differently endowed with resources, skills, and preferences; it is these differences which give rise to exchange. Thus a rancher who dislikes and is unskilled at the practice of medicine may exchange beef for the services of someone who is skilled in medicinal practice, but less than adept at raising beef. Both individuals will benefit as a result. This exchange need not involve direct barter, but can involve large numbers of other parties operating through the market system of a money economy.

This process of exchange is fundamental to economics as well as to economies. Individuals engage in exchange because they expect benefits. Provided there are no unexpected and unpleasant surprises, it is a game at which everyone wins. Because exchange is a mutually advantageous activity, the economic definition of an "efficient" allocation of society's resources is one in which it is not possible to find additional potential exchanges; i.e., each individual is as well off as he or she can be, given preferences and wealth. This exchange process is illustrated for the watershed economy in Figure 3.1. Consumers ultimately own labor, capital, and land, the factors of production in the economy. Consumers in the region provide these as services to local firms and to local governments; they receive wages, rents, and profits in return. These are represented by the flows shown between local consumers and local firms and governments in Figure 3.1. Remaining within the watershed system boundaries shown, these consumers can save some of their income in local financial institutions, earning interest, and purchase goods and services from local firms and governments, paying for these with consumption and tax expenditures, as shown. Local governments and firms use these receipts, together with capital from local financial institutions, to provide more goods and services, generating more income, and thus more demand. The watershed system is a complete and sustainable economic system.

Exchange with other regions — withdrawals

But just as individuals are differently endowed with preferences and skills, so are regions. The watershed, for example, is better suited to the production of beef than of coffee; trade with other regions will increase economic welfare. Interregional exchange is illustrated in Figure 3.1 by arrows crossing the system boundary. Arrows leading out of the system represent withdrawals; this money is taken out of the flow of income within the system, and thus reduces that flow. Arrows leading into the system represent flows of money into it from outside, or injections. By introducing new income into the system, these increase the flow of income within it.

Money can be withdrawn from the system by any of three sets of institutions shown in Figure 3.1. Consumers can purchase goods and services

*This section is based on Timothy Tregarthen, "Urbanizing Rural Land: Markets and Politics," paper prepared for Food, Fuel, and Shelter Conference.

from firms outside the region, put savings in external financial institutions, or pay taxes to external governments. An "external" government is one with boundaries beyond the region of interest. In the case of the watershed, this would include local counties to the extent that their monies were spent on services for constituents outside the watershed.

Local financial institutions generate withdrawals by lending money to individuals, firms, or governments outside the system. Local firms and governments often hire factors of production from outside the system; this would be the case for a watershed farmer hiring a laborer from Greeley. These external factors of production result in flows of wages, rents, and profits to agents outside the system. Similarly, local firms and governments purchase goods and services from outside the system; local firms pay taxes to external governments. All of these activities which withdraw money from the system, taken by themselves, reduce the flow of income within the system.

Injections

But if the "rest of the world," i.e. everything outside the system or region being considered, withdraws money from it, it also injects money back in. Each of these injections increases the flow of income within the system. Local consumers receive injections from outside the system by providing factors of production to external firms, financial institutions, and governments. Thus a resident of Elizabeth who works in Denver represents an export acitivity for the watershed, resulting in an external flow of income into the local economy, increasing the flow within the system. Local financial institutions receive savings from outside the system, and also receive interest payments on debts locally held.

Local governments and firms typically account for the bulk of income from outside the system. Firms sell goods and services to external agents; external agents invest in local firms, and local governments receive money from external governments, e.g. federal education aid and revenue sharing. All activities which involve an increase in injections increase the flow of income within the regional economy. Increases in withdrawals reduce it. Equality in injection and withdrawal demand results in an equilibrium level of regional income.

New Jobs

The export sector of the regional economy — the set of activities which generate injections of income into the system — is often regarded as the economic base of the system. An increase in employment in this sector generates additional local employment to provide for the needs of the new people in the expanded export sector. An increase in watershed wheat production as a result of increased world demand for wheat, for example, would increase employment in the economic base. These new workers would require additional local services, providing additional employment for grocers, insurance sales people, orthodontists, or whatever. By determining the relationship between employment in the economic base and total employment, it is possible to estimate the number of new local jobs that would be created by an increase in export employment. Preliminary analysis of the Elbert County economy, for example, suggests that each new job in the export sector induces approximately one additional local job; growth in the economic base is thus doubled in terms of its economic impact.

Timothy D. Tregarthen

While much more work would be required to compute the degree to which added jobs in the watershed's export sector increase total employment (the "multiplier effect"), some observations can be made. Because this watershed economy is heavily concentrated in agriculture, and because there is relatively little "support" employment within the watershed to support this base, the multiplier effect of increased export activities is likely to be small — probably on the order of that for Elbert County. But as development on the watershed continues, and the economy relies less on externally produced goods and services, this multiplier effect will begin to increase. Increases in export activity ten years from now will have a stronger effect on employment than they would today.

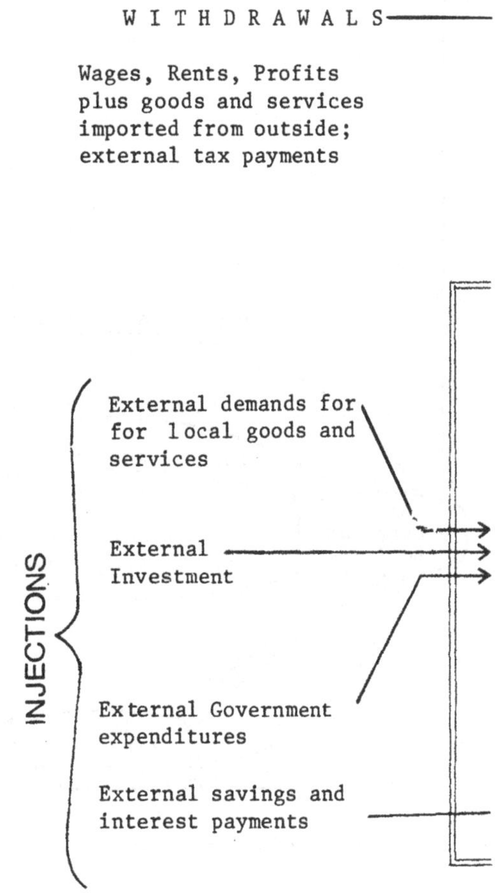

Fig. 3.1 The Exchange Process of the Watershed Economy

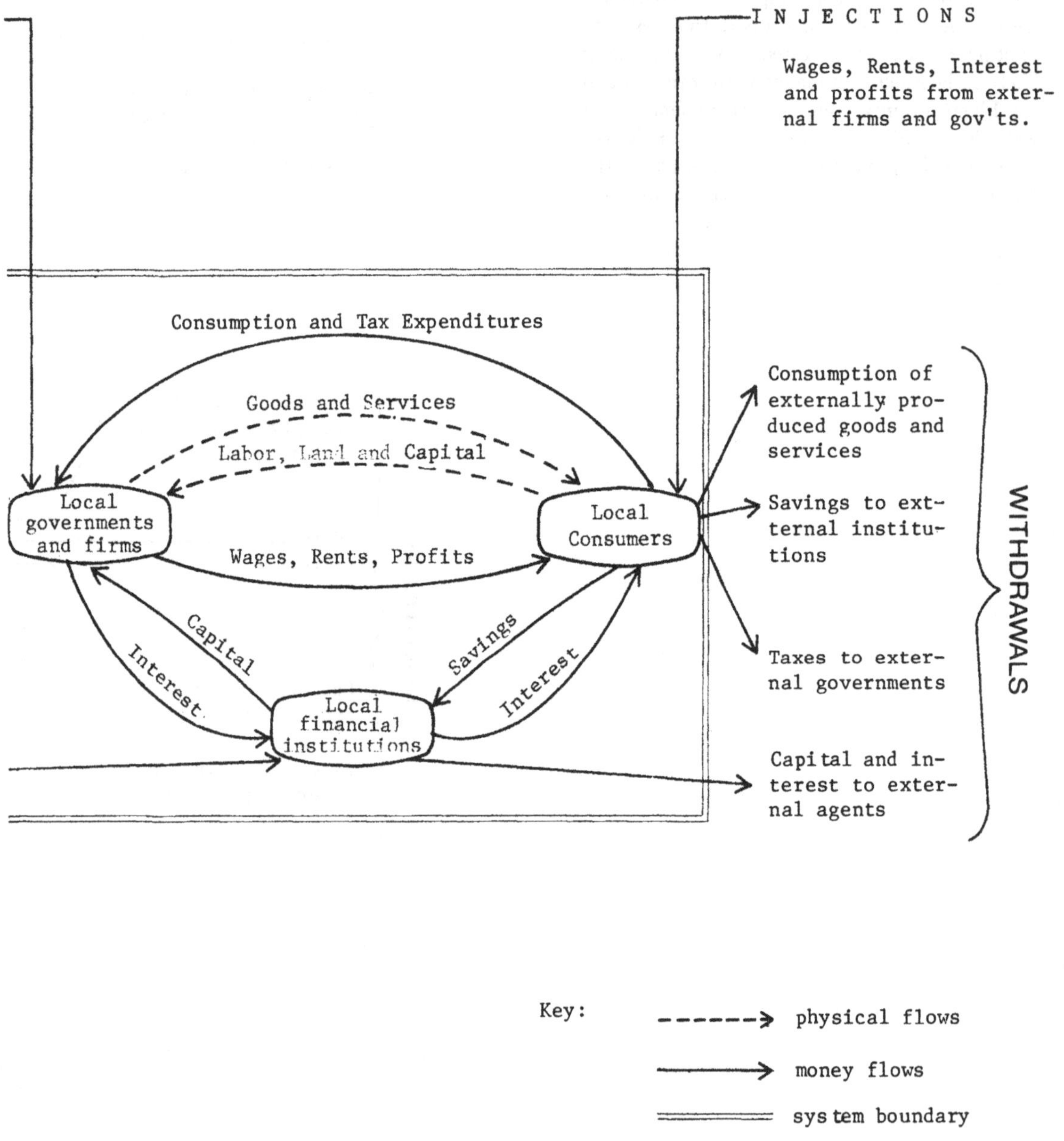

Economic Growth and Incomes*

Growth is an oft-cited goal for local and regional economic systems. Most advocates of growth today are somewhat more restrained in their enthusiasm for growth than they once were; growth goals now have a more qualitative dimension, reflecting increasing concern for the quality of life that people experience. But aside from concerns about the possible relationship between growth and crime, pollution, congestion, cost of public services, and the rest of the litany of urban complaints, there are significant limitations on the effects growth can have on economic factors in a regional system.

Wages

It is unlikely, for example, that economic growth in a system like that of the watershed will have any substantial effect on wages. To be sure, total income received by workers will rise — there will be more workers. But the watershed is an extremely small part of a much larger system with which it is closely integrated — the U.S. economy. Wages for any occupation in the watershed cannot for any long time differ greatly from wages for that occupation elsewhere. Higher watershed wages would attract more workers, bringing relative wages back down. This elimination of the differential need not require an absolute reduction in the higher watershed wage; the surplus of workers generated by it might simply prevent local wages from rising while national wages catch up. Similarly, watershed wages below those prevailing in the national system will induce local workers to leave, driving wages back up.

The notion of wages in this discussion must be interpreted broadly. Individuals are responsive not only to monetary wages available in an area, but to the quality of life in that area as well. Living in an unusually pleasant area generates satisfaction; individuals will be willing to work in such an area for a lower money wage than they would require elsewhere. The non-monetary rewards of a congenial situation must thus be considered along with money income in considering the real wage available in a region. Similarly, money wages must be adjusted to reflect regional differences in prices.

Real total wages — money wages adjusted for quality of life and price level differences — must be roughly equal among regions in the long run. Some differences might be sustained over time because of limits on the mobility of the work force imposed by transportation costs and imperfect information. But the U.S. labor force is hardly characterized by its immobility; real wage differentials sustained by these factors are unlikely to be large.

*This section is based on Timothy Tregarthen, "Urbanizing Rural Land: Markets and Politics," paper prepared for Food, Fuel, and Shelter Conference.

Unemployment

Growth in the economic base of a region is unlikely to result in a substantial reduction in the rate of unemployment for the same reasons cited above for the tendency toward equality in the real wages of specific occupations. Growth clearly generates more jobs, but it also generates an increase in the number of people seeking them. Unless it is physically, or perhaps culturally, isolated from the rest of the economy, no one region can long sustain an unemployment rate greatly different from that of the rest of the nation.

Profits

Finally, growth is unlikely to affect long run profits in most sectors of the regional economy. Substantial differences in rates of return on invested capital, adjusted for risk, cannot long persist between regions of the country; the existence of such differences would generate flows of investment that would eliminate them. Growth in the watershed economy might, for example, make existing grocery stores more profitable. But this increase in profitability must ultimately attract more grocery stores, driving profits back down to an equilibrium with the rest of the economy. This will not hold for sectors characterized by monopoly in which new firms cannot enter; profits for monopoly firms may increase with growth. Once again, the notion of profit must be adjusted for regional quality of life factors, or the psychological rewards of the activity itself. Thus a farmer might accept a low monetary rate of return on investment because he or she enjoys the lifestyle offered by farming.

Growth does affect the character of a region. It expands the range of consumption and employment opportunities. It may also increase pollution and congestion. Residents of Denver have an excellent symphony; residents of Elizabeth have clean air to breathe. But the effect of growth on individual incomes is less significant than is commonly thought. A local economy cannot separate itself from the rest of the world, and thus can do little about rates of wages, profits, and unemployment.

Buford Rice

Agricultural Operations: Grazing*

Agriculture is the dominant economic activity on the watershed; it is the main component of the system's economic base. It is therefore useful to examine watershed agricultural practices in some detail. The likely effects of urbanization on agriculture will be considered in Chapter Four. The analysis here begins with livestock grazing operations. The next section deals with dryland and irrigated crops. The distribution of these activities on the watershed is shown in Figure 3.2.

Table 3.1 gives the distribution of livestock for the four watershed counties; cattle dominate this list. Watershed ranchers graze cattle on pastures in preparation for final fattening at the feedlot. Grazing operations rely heavily on the natural as well as the economic system. In particular, there are four principles of sound livestock management that rely on these factors:

1. The class of stock must be carefully selected on the basis of available forage, topography, soils, and market conditions. The shortgrass prairie system described in Chapter Two is particularly well adapted for cattle.
2. Seasonal variations must be observed. The cool season/warm season mix of watershed grasslands discussed in Chapter Two allows year-round grazing.

*These sections are based on George M. Van Dyne, "Renewable Resource Systems of the Running Creek (Box Elder) Area."

Fig. 3.2 Major Agricultural Activities on the Watershed

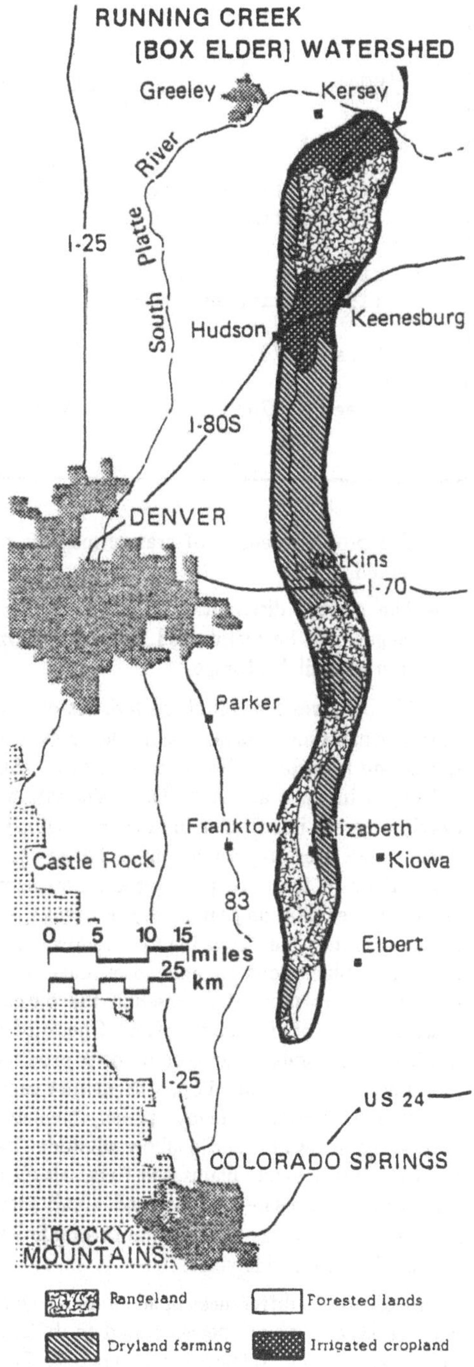

Table 3.1 Livestock in Watershed Counties

Item	COUNTY Adams	Arapahoe	Elbert	Weld	COLORADO (% of State total)
Livestock	(number in thousands)				
all cattle and calves (1975 estimates)	52.0	20.0	52.0	588.0	3375.0 (21%)
milk cows (1975 estimates	4.4	0.4	1.7	22.7	75.0 (39%)
hogs (1973)	18.0	0.8	3.6	43.0	290.0 (23%)
sheep (1974)	4.0	1.0	1.6	16.0	630.0 (3.6%)

3. The proper intensity of grazing must be observed.
4. The correct distribution of animals over a range must be maintained to assure utilization of available forage.

Table 3.2 gives the soil characteristics of range sites in Adams and Arapahoe counties. Figure 3.3 shows the location of broad categories of these soil types in the watershed. This information is clearly of great importance in range management. Some range sites are, for example, better suited than others in terms of plant production in unfavorable precipitation years. Gravel breaks, wet meadows, sandy meadows, loamy meadow slopes, and loamy plains soils are able to produce in unfavorable years more than one-half the biomass characteristics of favorable years. One-third to one-half of favorable year production is produced in unfavorable years on choppy sands, dry sands, sandy bottomlands, clayey plains, sandstone breaks, plains swales, and shallow siltstone sites. Siltstone plains, sandy plains, salt flats, salt meadows, overflows, shaley plains, and alkali plains provide less than one-third of the favorable year biomass in unfavorable years.

In addition to differences in adaptability to climate variations, plant species found in different soil types respond differently to grazing. Table 3.3 gives the typical distribution of plant species by range site type for the watershed. Some species, such as blue grama and fringed sagewort, are considered "increasing" species because they increase in concentration in an area under heavy grazing. Blue grama is successful under these conditions because its growing stem is typically below the range of feeding cattle. Other species, termed "decreasers" because their concentration in the plant community declines under heavy grazing, include Junegrass, mountain muhly, western wheatgrass, and needlegrass. Decreasers on sandy soils include sand bluestem, needle-and-thread, little bluestem, and side oats grama. Tall grass sites with overflow waters have Indian grass, switchgrass, and big bluestem as decreasers, while clay textured soils have four-winged saltbrush and winterfat as decreasers. These latter species are difficult to maintain even under moderate grazing.

Succession

Changing climatological or economic conditions may force the abandonment of cropland; such abandonment triggers a process of succession in the plant community that follows a predictable pattern. In the initial stage after abandonment, the community is dominated by Russian thistle, pigweed, lambsquarter, and other annuals. This is followed by a forb stage dominated by a wide variety of annual and perennial forbs,

Table 3.2 General characteristics of some important range sites in Adams and Arapahoe counties (SCS Technical Guide Range Site Descriptions for the Central High Plains Land Resource Area. Col. SCS, U.S.D.A., 1975).

	LOAMY PLAINS	LOAMY SLOPES
Slope %	0-10	5-15
Elevation	4000-5700	4500-5500
Landform Characteristics	sloping tableland	catsteps
Precipitation, centimeters	33-43	33-36
Ground Cover, percent	35	NA
Yield Maximum, kg/ha	8250	6600
Yield Minimum, kg/ha	4950	3850

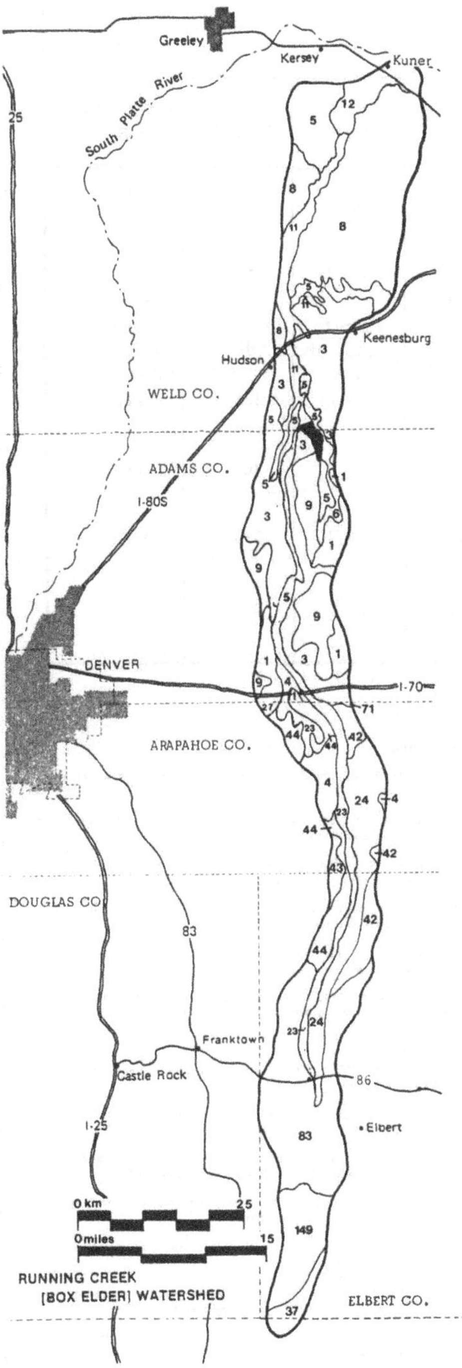

Fig. 3.3 Major Soil Type Associations on the Watershed (from SCS Soil Surveys for Watershed Counties)

DEEP SANDS	SANDY PLAINS	SALT FLAT	OVERFLOW	GRAVEL BREAKS	WET MEADOW	CLAYEY PLAINS	ALKALINE PLAINS	SANDSTONE BREAKS
3-20	0-10	0	0	0-20	0	NA	0-5	9-45
4000-5500	3800-5000	3000-6000	3000-6000	4000 6000	3000-6000	5500-	3300-6200	4000-6500
sloping to undulating	level to rolling	low-lying bottom-lands	sloping to level	gravelly hills and rough	level to sloping	terrace to steep side slopes	gentle rolling to level	rough and broken steep slope
33-43	33-43	25-48	33-48	33-48	33-43	25-38	33-43	33-43
40	40	25	50-55	60	40	25	30	30
13750	13750	9900	19250	22000	7150	11000	5500	6600
6600	4400	2750	5500	16500	3300	2750	2450	3850

WELD CO.

3 WELD-COLBY: deep, level to gently sloping, well drained loam soils; formed in calcareous eolian deposits

5 OLNEY-KIM-OTERO: deep, nearly level to moderately sloping, well drained sandy loam and loam soils; formed in mixed alluvium and eolian deposits

8 VALENT-VONA-OSGOOD: deep, nearly level to moderately sloping, well to excessively drained sand and sandy loam soils; formed in eolian deposits

11 NUNN-HAVERSON: deep, level to nearly level, well drained loam and clay loam soils formed in alluvium

12 NUNN-DACONO-ALTVAN: deep, level to nearly level, well drained loam and clay loam soils; formed in alluvium

ADAMS CO.

1 WELD-ADENA-COLBY: nearly level to steep, well drained, loamy soils formed in wind-laid deposits; on uplands

3 ASCALON-VONA-TRUCKTON: nearly level to strongly sloping, well-drained and somewhat excessively drained, loamy and sandy soils formed in wind-laid deposits; on uplands

4 NUNN-SATANTA: nearly level, well-drained, loamy soils formed in alluvial materials that are underlain by gravel in some places; on terraces and fans

5 ALLUVIAL LAND: nearly level, poorly drained to well-drained loamy and sandy soils formed in stream and river deposits; on flood plains

6 TERRY-RENOHILL-TASSEL: Gently sloping to steep, well-drained and somewhat excessively drained, loamy soils formed in materials from soft sandstone and shale; on uplands

9 PLATNER-ULM-RENOHILL: nearly level to strongly sloping, well-drained, loamy soils formed in old alluvium on interbedded shale and sandstone; on uplands

ARAPAHOE CO.

23 NUNN-FORT COLLINS: Warm, deep, well drained, nearly level soils on terraces

27 WELD-ADENA-COLBY: Warm, deep, well drained, nearly level and gently sloping soils on upland plains

42 NUNN-BRESSER-ASCALON: Warm, deep, well drained, nearly level and gently sloping soils on upland plains

43 STAPLETON-BRESSER-NEWLIN: Warm, deep, well drained, gently sloping and moderately steep soils on upland plains

44 FONDIS-WELD: Warm, deep, well drained, nearly level and gently sloping soils on upland plains

71 ASCALON-VONA-TRUCKTON: Warm, deep, well drained and somewhat excessively drined, nearly level to sloping soils on upland plains

ELBERT CO.

23 NUNN-FORT COLLINS: Warm, deep, well drained, nearly level soils on terraces

24 TRUCKTON-BRESSER-BLAKELAND: Warm, deep, well drained, nearly level and gently sloping soils on upland plains and terraces

37 KETTLE-PRING-PEYTON: Cool, deep, well and somewhat excessively drained, gently sloping and sloping soils on upland plains

42 NUNN-BRESSER-ASCALON: Warm, deep, well drained, nearly level and gently sloping soils on upland plains

44 FONDIS-WELD: Warm, deep, well drained, nearly level and gently sloping soils on upland plains

83 FONDIS-KUTCH: Warm, deep and moderately deep, well drained, nearly level and sloping soils on upland plains

149 BRUSSETT-JARRE: Cool, deep, well drained, gently sloping to moderately steep soils on upland plains

Table 3.3 Species in Selected Range sites in Northeastern Colorado.

(SCS Technical Guide Range Sight Descriptions for the Central High Plains Land Resource Area. Col. SCS, U.S.D.A., 1975).

Numerical data represents maximum percent composition by weight, T indicates trace, and x indicates the species is an invader

	LOAMY* PLAINS	LOAMY* SLOPES	SILTSTONE PLAINS	PLAINS SWALE	DEEP* SAND	CHOPPY SAND	SANDY* PLAINS	SANDY MEADOW	SANDY BOTTOMLAND	SALT* FLAT	SALT MEADOW	OVERFLOW*	SALINE OVERFLOW	WET MEADOWS	SHALLOW SILTSTONE	CLAYEY* PLAINS	ALKALINE* PLAINS	SANDSTONE PLAINS	GRAVEL PLAINS
Grasses and Grasslike Plants											10								
alkali bluegrass								5		45	45		35			7	40		
alkali sacaton											10								
Baltic rush												10		15					T
blowout grass						10													
blue grama	65	55	50	10	10		10			30		15	25		50	30	20		20
bottlebrush squirreltail	5															5	5		
buffalograss	5	3	5	5						5			5				2		
Canada wildrye									5		5			5					
cheatgrass brome												x							
foxtail barley								x			3			5					
galleta										25			5			5	15		
grama grasses						5													
green needlegrass																7			T
June grass							5												5
Indian ricegrass						5													5
inland saltgrass				5					3	10	15								
little bluestem	2	3					10		5						2				15
native bluegrass								5											
needle and thread	5	3	5		15	15	10		5				5		3				5
nuttall albaligrass										20									
prairie cordgrass								2						15					
prairie sandreed					25	20	5	21	12			5							10
pullup muhly						1													
red three-awn	5	x	T												x				
ring muhly	T	x																	
sand bluestem					15	25	1	15	15										
sand dropseed	5	2	5				10						5		10				5
sandhill muhly						5													
sedges	5	1		5			5		3		10					3			5
sedges and rushes								6						10					
sideoats grama	3	3				10	20		5			5			2				10
silver bluestem													5						
slender wheatgrass											5	5							
switchgrass						5	1	21	25		20	20	5	20					
tall dropseed																			
threadleaf sedge															3				
tumblegrass	x	x	T																
vine mesquite										5			10						
western wheatgrass	10	20	20	70				10	3	20	20	15	25		10	25	5		
wheat grasses														15					
yellow Indiangrass							1					10		10					
other grasses					5			10	10				10	15					

	LOAMY* PLAINS	LOAMY* SLOPES	SILTSTONE PLAINS	PLAIN SWALE	DEEP* SAND	CHOPPY SAND	SANDY* PLAINS	SANDY MEADOW	SANDY BOTTOMLAND	SALT* FLAT	SALT MEADOW	OVERFLOW*	SALINE OVERFLOW	WET* MEADOW	SHALLOW SILTSTEON	CLAYEY* PLAINS	SHALEY PLAINS	ALKALINE* PLAIN	SANDSTONE* BREAKS	GRAVEL* BREAKS
Forbs																				
American vetch				2																
annual buckwheat						X														
buffaloburr nightshade				X																
Canada thistle												X								
cockleburr				X																
cudweed sagewort																				
curlycup gunweed										X	X					X				
fanweed	X																			
frankenia																	5			
fremont goldenrod																		X		
kochia				T				X	X	X	X	X		X	X					
loco	X	X																		
mouse-eared povertyweed																				
musk thistle												X						X		
povertyweed					X						X									
prairie clover																				5
redroot pigweed					X							X								
Russian knapweed												X								
Russian thistle	X	X		T	X	X			X	X	X	X			X					
showy pigweed					X	X														
small-pod loco				1																
stickweed whitetoo				X								X								
suckleya				X																
sunflower					X	X														
sweat pea				2																
thistle	X																			
wild alfalfa	T	T																		
wild licorice											2									
annual weeds																		X		
other perennial forbs		5	T																	5
forbs						10			3	10	5	15					10			
annual forbs				X					X							X				
Shrubs and Half-Shrubs																				
broom snakeweed	T	T	T												X					
four-wing saltbrush			10							10	5	5	10		5	9	5	5		T
fringed sagewort	T	T																		5
greasewood											2			X			X	X		
rabbitbrush			T							3				X						
sand sagebrush					10	5														
winterfat			5							5					15	3	5	3		5
yucca					3	5											X			T
Cactus																				
cholla cactus																		X		
pricklypear cactus	T	T				X					X							X		
Trees																				
cottonwood								3												
marsh elder														X						
tamarex								X	X	X	X									

*** Designates range sites found on Running Creek Watershed**

together with a few grasses. If the succession is permitted to continue, a short-lived perennial grass community will develop, in which tumblegrass, little barley, sand dropseed, and bottlebrush squirreltail are abundant. Dense stands of red three-awn grasses dominate the fourth stage, followed by a final stage characterized by a full developed stand of shortgrasses, midgrasses, forbs, and shrubs. The entire process may require more than fifty years to complete. Drouth will retard this cycle; wet periods will accelerate it. A return to heavy grazing may also retard the process; indeed, it may terminate succession indefinitely at the forb and short-lived perennial grass stage.

A similar cycle has been observed for abandoned cropland in the ponderosa pine community southwest of the southern end of the watershed. The first one to three years were characterized by annual forbs, especially lambsquarter, sunflower, nightshade, and crown beard. These species provide poor soil protection and low quality herbage for grazing. The annuals of the first stage were followed by perennial forbs and grasses — fringed sagewort, wormwood sagewort, fleabane, bull thistle, tumblegrass, and toadflax. These herbs dominated for one to three years, followed by another one to three year cycle of mixed grasses and weeds. This phase, which could be maintained indefinitely under heavy grazing, included big needlegrass, green needlegrass, slender wheatgrass, Junegrass, Kentucky bluegrass, western wheatgrass, mountain muhly, nodding brome, Arkansas rose, fleabane, and fringed sagewort. The final phase featured western yarrow, pussytoe, locoweed, blue grama, mountain muhly, Arizona fescue, and threadleaf sedge. Additional experiments with succession are in progress at Running Creek Field Station.

Given the soil type and mix of plant species, the question of intensity of grazing presents one of the key decision variables facing ranchers. It is also one of the most difficult. In general, it may be desirable to avoid close grazing during April, May, and June in shortgrass areas of the watershed to avoid depletion of the cool season species that permit year-round operations. Grazing should be controlled to maintain blue grama in coarse textured soils; blue grama and buffalograss should be maintained on fine textured soils.

More precise specification of grazing intensity is difficult for the watershed. Plant production varies with precipitation, also a highly variable factor. Attempts to develop a figure for grazing animals per hectare based on the peak standing crop in an area miss the important feature of watershed phenology — the differing timing of the growth of plant species. Summing the biomass of the peaks for each species gives a total biomass as much as three times that found by taking a single measure of the peak standing crop reached during the season. An alternative approach that appears to be more useful is to determine the amount of biomass needed to be left standing at the end of the season to maximize annual returns; this has been estimated to be about 340 kilograms per hectare.

A 20 year study for northeastern Colorado* provided the data for Figure 3.4 showing the relationship between hectares per yearling heifer per month and weight gain. Gains per animal increase up to 1.2 hectares per heifer, then decline. Gains per hectare peak at .9 hectares per heifer per month. The maximization of kilograms gained per hectare is not by itself an adequate criterion; the price received for each animal is a function of its condition. For the watershed as a whole, carrying capacities of grazing land range from 6-8 hectares per year per animal to 14 hectares per year per animal at the drier northern end. These capacities can be varied, of course, with supplemental feeding. Acreage near the creek is more productive than that of the sandy or clayey loam characteristic of upland sites.

Minimum costs per unit of beef produced require an operation of at least 200-300 cattle. Taking a figure of ten hectares per animal and a 250 head operation, a minimum unit of 2500 hectares is required — an area equal to about 2 percent of the watershed.

A further consideration in range management is calving; strategies that increase the calf crop will increase the profitability of ranching operations. One approach is to provide improved nutrition for heifers, allowing them to be calved at age two. This requires wintering calves to gain at least .2 kilograms per day. The addition of extra cool season grasses may increase the calf crop by ten percent. Watershed ranches do well with reseeding of crested wheatgrass, intermediate wheatgrass, Russian wildrye, tall wheatgrass, and green needlegrass. At the southern end of the watershed, in

*Bement, R.E. 1971, "Implementing Range Management." *Range Beef-Cow Symposium* (Cheyenne, Wyoming, 13-15 December 1971) *Proceedings* pp. 95-97.

Fig. 3.4 Impact of stocking rate over 19 years on northeastern Colorado shortgrass prairie rangeland on sandy loam soils in a 25 to 38 centimeter precipitation zone. (Based on data from Bement 1971)

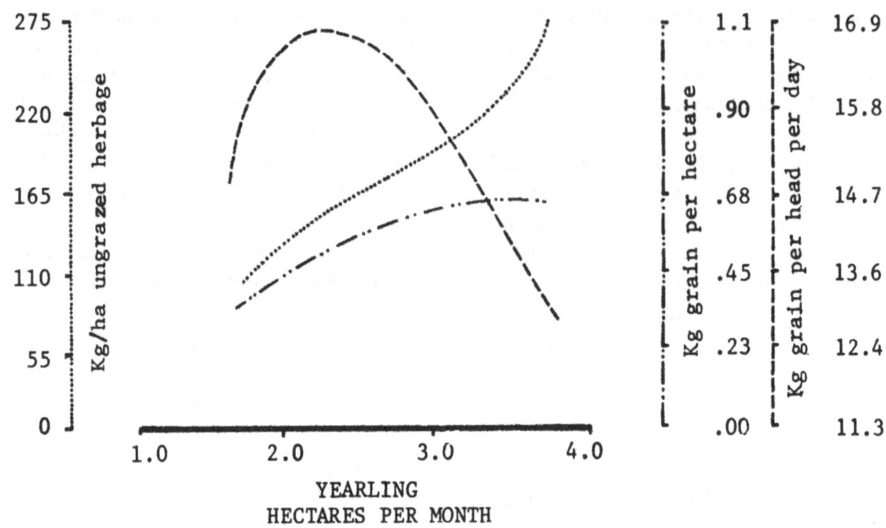

Fig. 3.5 Cattle, Plants and Animals: A Feedback Loop

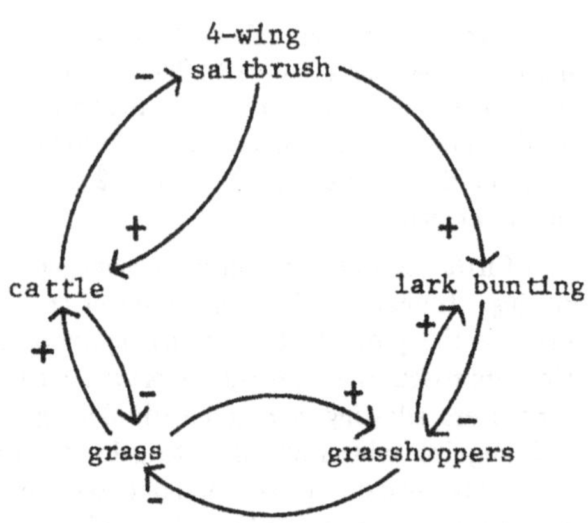

Arrows show the direction of casualty. Plus signs indicate that there is a positive relation; minus signs indicate a negative relation.

Fig. 3.6 Water Run-off and Grazing on Shortgrass Prairie in Northeastern Colorado

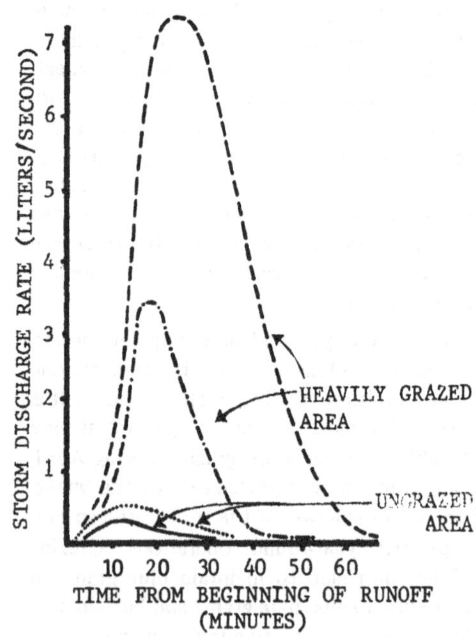

Hydrographs for a midsummer storm on shortgrass prairie in northeastern Colorado (From Striffler, 1971).

Fig. 3.7 Energy Flow in the Shortgrass Prairie

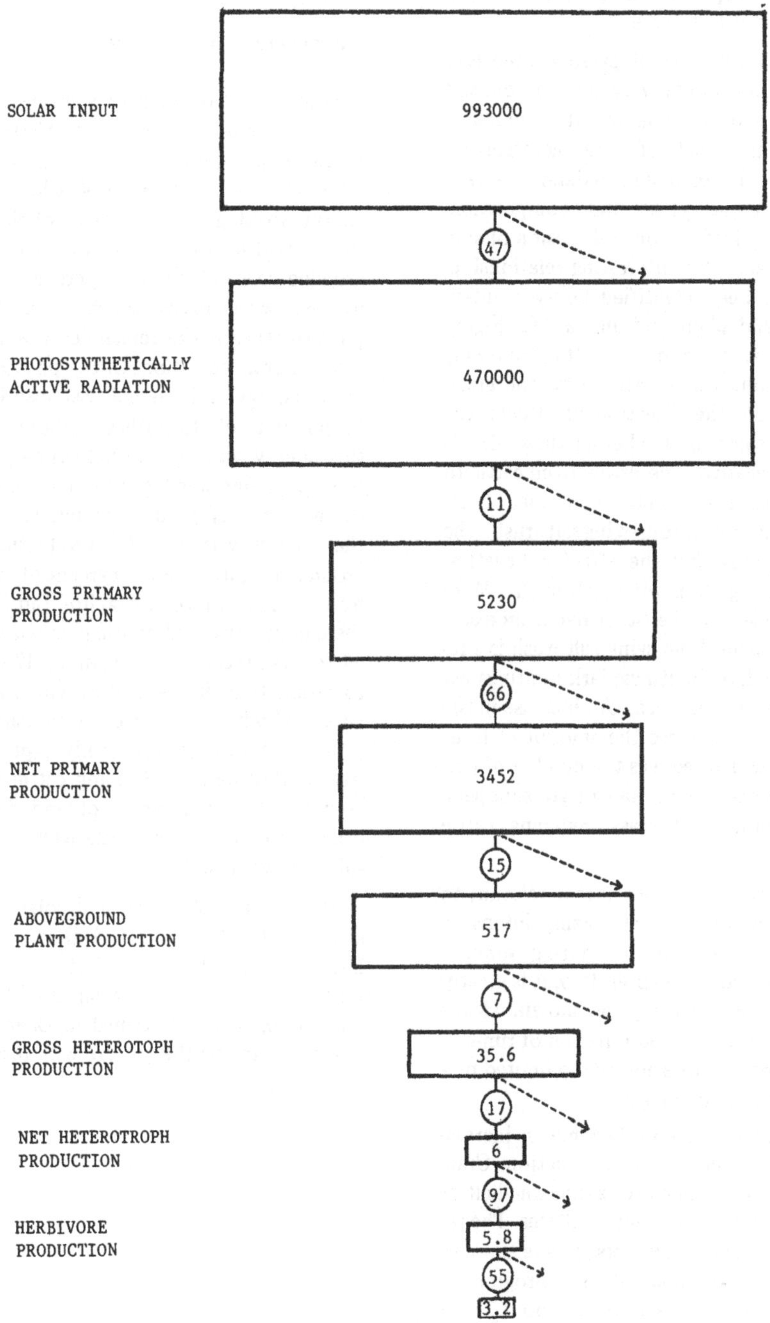

Estimates for energy flow into and through various components in the shortgrass prairie (based on data from Coleman et al., 1976)

higher rainfall areas, smooth brome and pubescent wheatgrass are useful. Finally, cross-bred cattle produce calf crops exceeding those of purebred cattle by about five percent.

The discussion thus far of grazing intensities has been based on the relatively small amount of research that has been done for the watershed region. Long term impacts of differing intensities of grazing need to be examined to determine relationships to herbage yield and composition, drouth, resistance, infiltration and erosion of soil, and wildlife impact. One interesting relationship, for example, has been identified between intensity of grazing and plant and animal life. Figure 3.5 shows a "feedback loop" for cattle, four-wing saltbrush, lark buntings, grasshoppers, and grass. The arrows denote the direction of effects; the plus and minus signs show whether these effects are positive or negative. The arrow from cattle to four-wing saltbrush shows that the number of cattle affects the amount of four-wing saltbrush. The minus sign indicates that the effect is negative; cattle enjoy eating four-wing saltbrush. More four-wing saltbrush, on the other hand, increases the amount of cattle. Four-wing saltbrush is a favored habitat of lark buntings; lark buntings eat grasshoppers — which eat grass. An increase in the intensity of grazing reduces the amount of four-wing saltbrush, which reduces the number of lark buntings, increasing the number of grasshoppers, reducing the amount of grass, reducing cattle gains.

Figure 3.6 suggests another factor relevant to the determination of optimal grazing intensity. The problem of water runoff during summer storms was discussed in Chapter Two; it is greatly intensified by heavy grazing, as shown. Heavy grazing increases the rate and duration of run-off, reducing further the utilization of the limited precipitation in a semi-arid climate.

The grazing of cattle may become an increasingly important source of beef production. Grazing operations now account for about one-half of the beef production in the United States. The remainder is generated in feedlots, where animals are fattened for market in an intensive program of grain feeding. This process requires about seven kilograms of grain for each kilogram of weight gain. If the relative cost of grain increases, as it may with rising world demand and energy costs, the percentage of beef production provided by grazing may rise — some observers estimate that it may go as high as 90 percent.

Solar energy used in grazing

Grazing is not an energy intensive activity in terms of its use of fossil fuels. Cattle do require, however, a good deal of solar energy. Figure 3.7 traces the fate of the 993,000 kilocalories of solar energy striking a square meter of shortgrass prairie in northeastern Colorado during a 154 day growing season.* Only 47 percent of this energy was in wavelengths which could be used for photosynthesis; the remainder was used to heat the soil and vegetation. Of the photosynthetically active energy, 1.1 percent was absorbed and used by plants in photosynthesis. About two-thirds of this energy was used in net primary production; the remainder was lost through transpiration. Of the net primary production figure, 15 percent of the energy was used for production of aboveground vegetation; seven percent of this was eaten by various forms of animal life. But 83 percent of the energy thus used by the plant eaters was needed for respiration. The remaining 17 percent went to production, 95 percent of which was by herbivores, of which 55 percent were cattle. The percentage of solar energy finally captured in cattle was .00032 percent. Grazing cattle is clearly an activity intensive in its use of land; despite its low utilization rate, it is a relatively heavy user of solar energy as well.

Historically, this land and solar energy intensive activity has been a logical response to a market in which these two factors were relatively quite cheap. Solar energy captured by plants will remain so; forces described in Chapter Four are already changing the picture with respect to land.

*Growing seasons for watershed counties average: Adams 160 days, Arapahoe 151 days, Elbert 142 days, and Weld 137 days. From: "Information on Colorado Agriculture," Colorado Dept. of Agriculture, Denver, 1974. Statistics are based on weather data for the period, 1941-1970.

Crop Production

The four watershed counties (not the watershed itself) together account for about 20 percent of the dollar value of field crop production in Colorado. Table 3.4 summarizes this production for 1973. This production represents both dryland and irrigated farming.

Winter wheat, the leading dryland crop in the region, has shown a four-fold increase in cubic meters per hectare since 1925. This gain reflects improvement in weather (from the drought years early in the period), technology, and genetic material. Yields in Elbert County now average 1.8 cubic meters per hectare; other counties on the watershed average 2.6. In addition to increasing yields in winter wheat production, there has been an increase in hectares devoted to it — a five-fold increase in Adams County alone. Most of this increase represents a conversion of pasture land.

Winter wheat is planted in the fall and harvested in the spring; a summer fallow period allows water storage in the soil. As much as one-third of annual precipitation can be retained for subsequent crop production in this manner. Figure 3.8 shows the importance of soil water plus precipitation for crop production. Adequate soil water can make the difference between getting by and disaster in a bad precipitation season.

Economizing on scarce water requires the use of an energy intensive approach of frequent tillages — perhaps four or five per season — for weed control. Both weeds and wheat require 500 kilograms of water per kilogram of dry matter produced. Control of weed growth in eastern Colorado may increase the storage of water in the soil by 2.5 to 5 centimeters and yields of wheat of 1.2 to 4 cubic meters per hectare. Similarly, straw yields can be increased by 550-1100 kilograms per hectare through weed control.

The behavior of the soil water system is of particular importance for all dryland crops, and, indeed, for irrigated crops as well. More than 60 percent of winter precipitation is lost to evaposublimation and wind transport of snow on upland sites. Vegetation plays a key role in the "trapping" of snow by the land — a stubble mulch increases this retention. Snow melt is important; as much as three-fourths of the soil water recharge on cropland may be due to snow melt.

Figures 3.9 to 3.16 give crop data for Adams County, and winter wheat data for all four watershed counties. Information is plotted at five or

Fig. 3.8 Water Availability and Winter Wheat Yields in Eastern Colorado

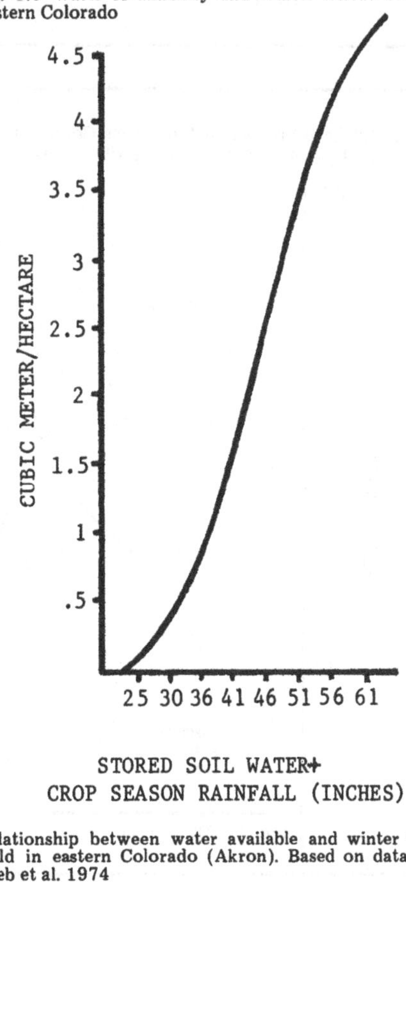

Relationship between water available and winter wheat yield in eastern Colorado (Akron). Based on data from Greb et al. 1974

Table 3.4 Crop Production in Watershed Counties and Colorado: 1973

Item	Adams	Arapahoe	Elbert	Weld	Colorado
	County				
Field Crops (1973)	(millions of dollars)				
winter wheat	14.000	5.4000	3.100	16.000	23.0
spring wheat	.180	.0130	-	.081	1.9
corn, grain	1.400	.1200	.170	15.000	113.0
corn, silage	1.600	.3200	.560	36.000	83.0
barley	.920	.3000	.260	3.100	26.0
sorghum	.086	.0240	.024	.034	23.0
dry beans	.12	-	.045	7.400	39.0
sugar beets	.47	-	-	20.000	66.0
oats	.054	.0044	.065	.390	2.8
hay	2.600	.7100	2.700	15.00	140.0
potatoes	-	-	-	2.30	49.0
other crops	2.600	.3600	.043	4.50	42.0
Total	24.000	7.200	7.000	119.00	817.0

Fig. 3.9 Crop production for Adams County, Colorado as derived from Colorado Agrigultural Statistics Reports. Note that the ordinate is scaled logarithmically.

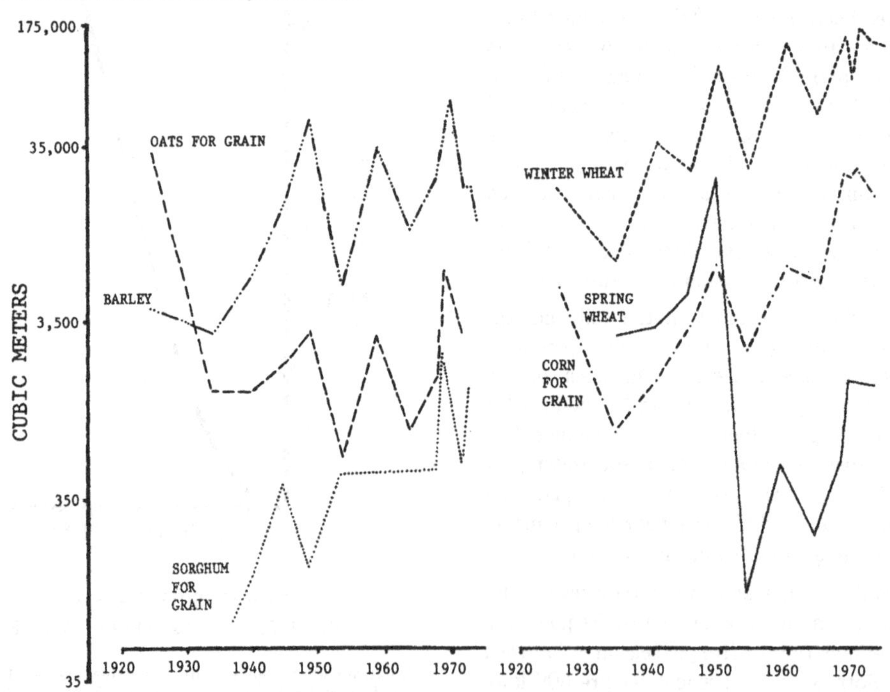

Fig. 3.10 Crop yields per hectare for Adams County, Colorado as derived from Colorado Agricultural Statistics Reports. Note that the ordinate is scaled logarithmically.

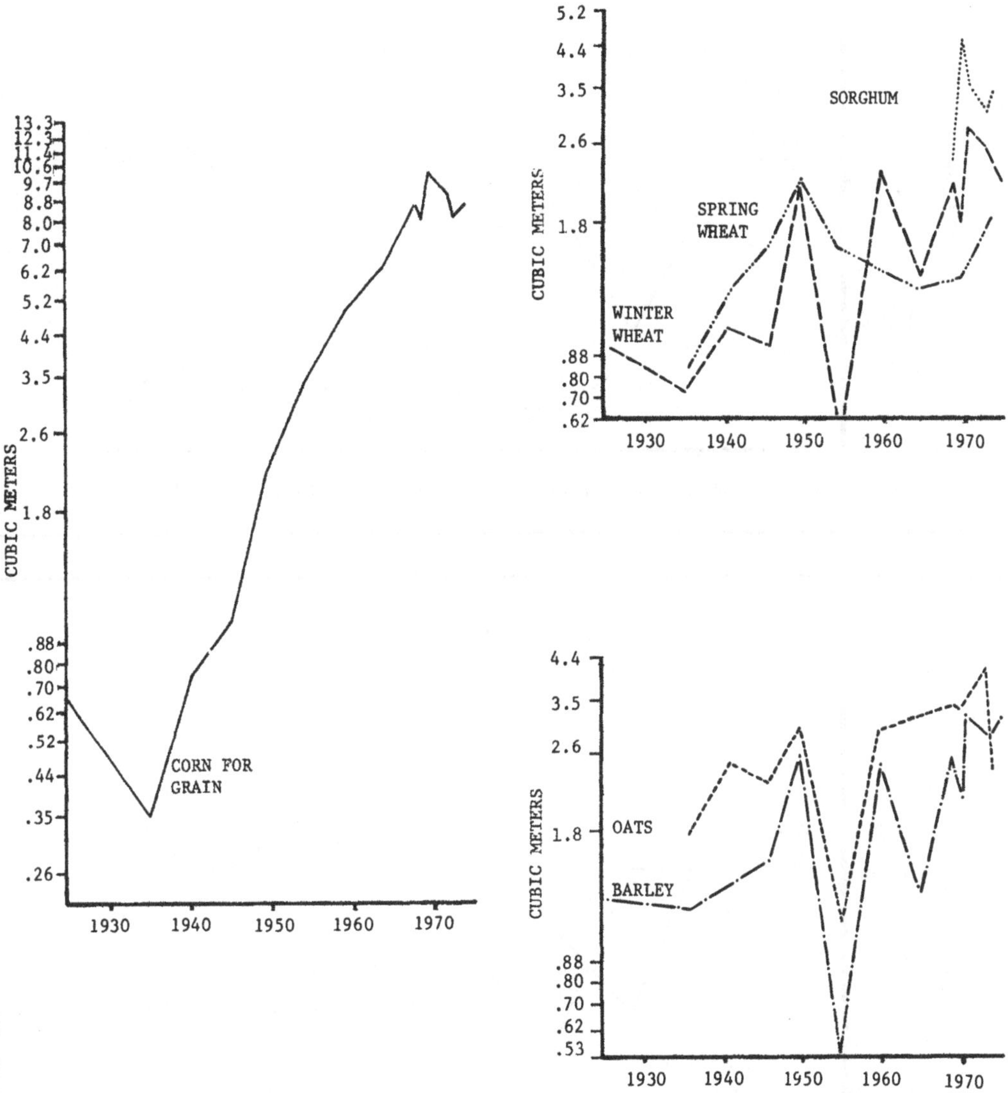

Fig. 3.11 Hectares of important crops in Adams County, Colorado as derived from Colorado Agricultural Statistics Reports. Note that the ordinate is scaled logarithmically.

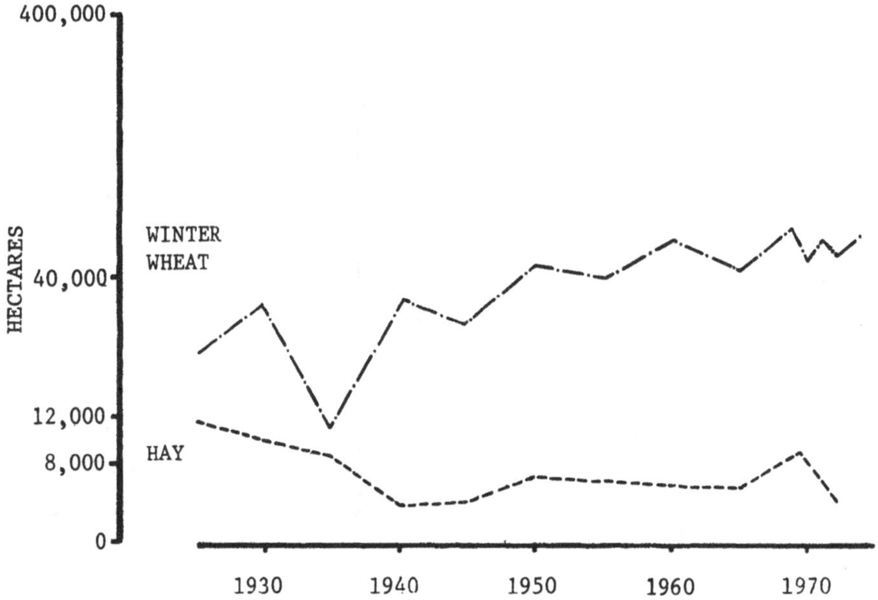

Fig. 3.12

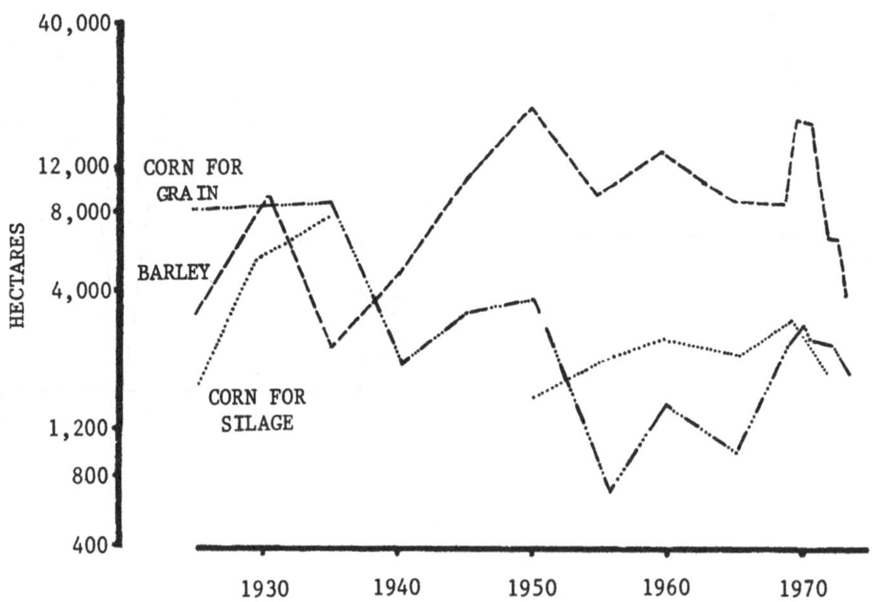

Fig. 3.13

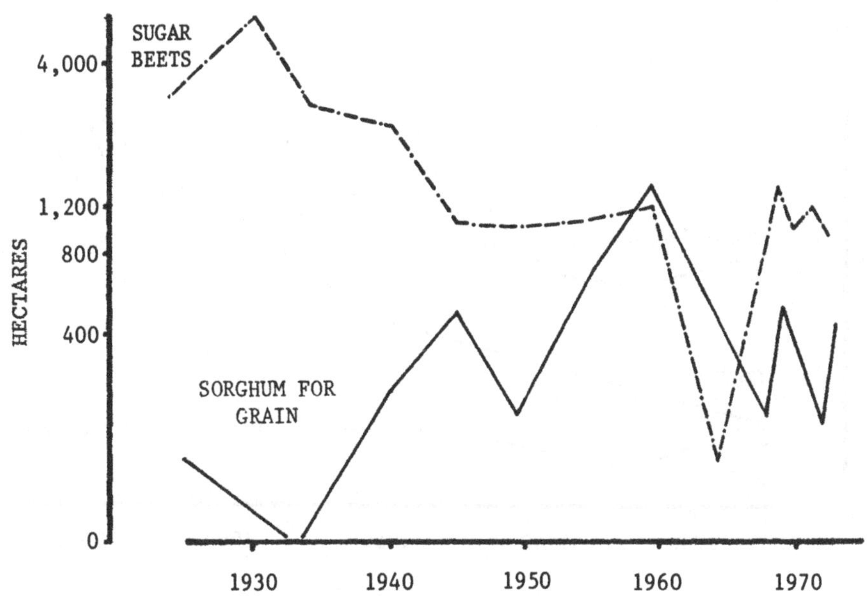

Fig. 3.14

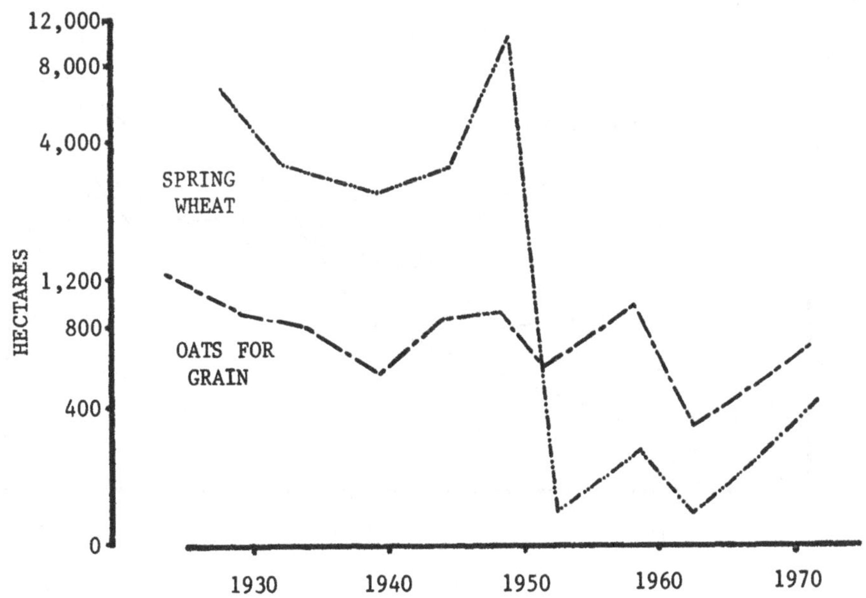

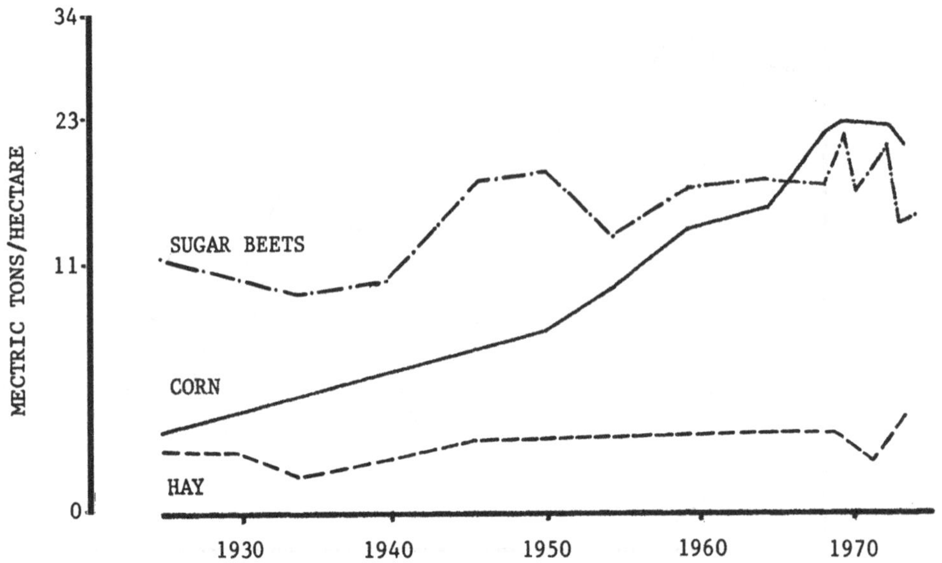

Fig. 3.15 Data for Adams County, Colorado, metric tons (lower graph) and metric tons per hectare (upper graph) for sugar beets, hay, and corn silage as derived from Colorado Agricultural Reports. Note that the ordinates are scaled logarithmically.

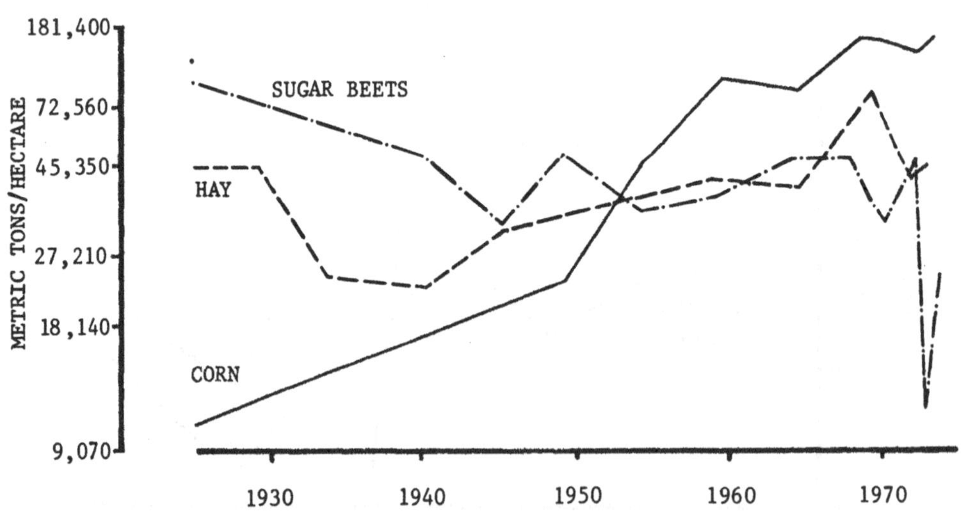

Fig. 3.16 Winter Wheat Production

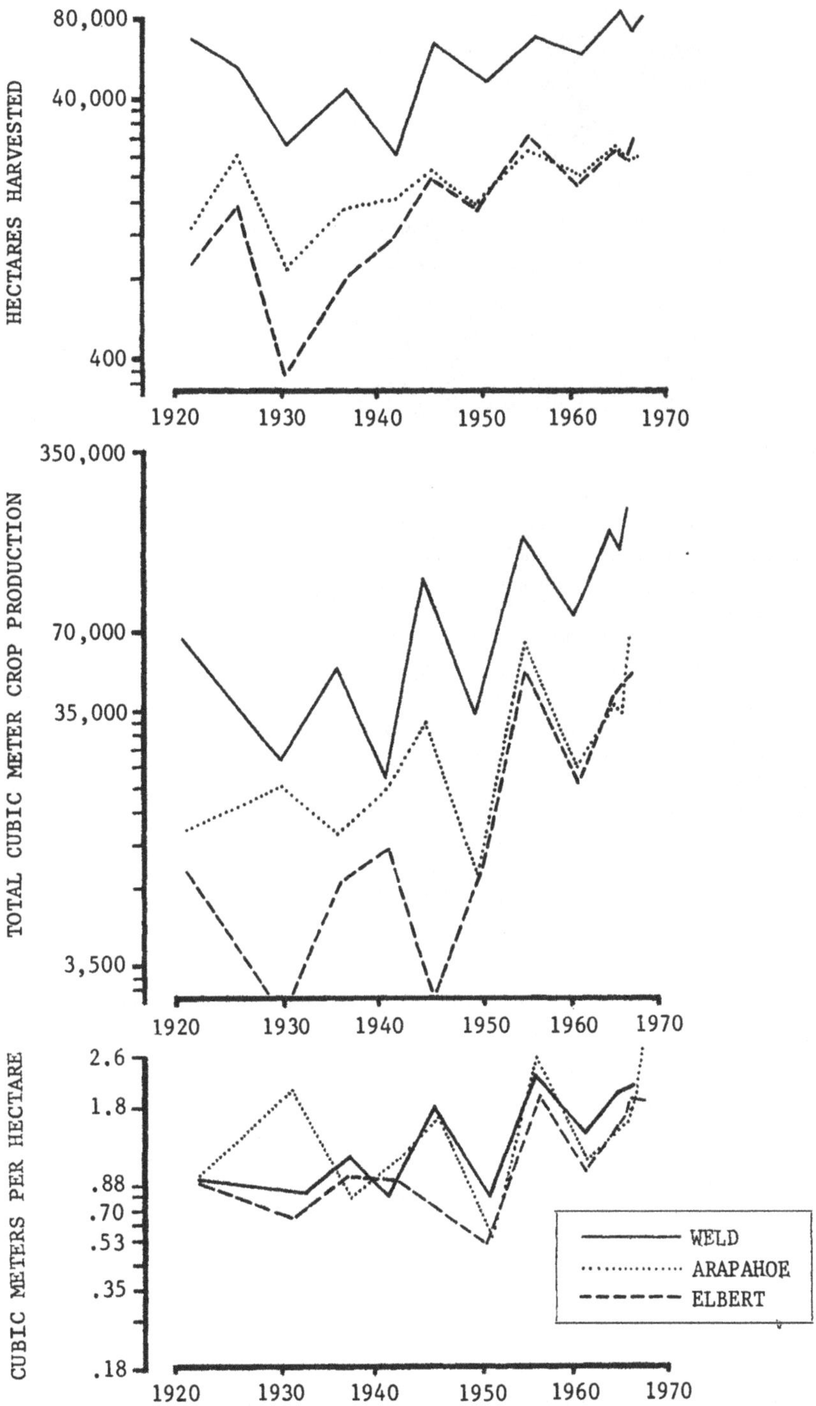

Winter wheat production, hectares, and yield per hectare for Weld, Arapahoe, and Elbert counties as derived from Colorado Agricultural Statistics Reports, 1974. Note that the ordinates are scaled logarithmically.

David Dechant

ten year intervals; lines connecting these points do not imply interpolation. After a long period of increases, yields per hectare appear to be leveling off in Adams County; this does not appear to be attributable to changing weather conditions.

Watershed agricultural operations are closely linked with the operation of the natural system. They are an integral part of the economic system; it is, in turn, a critical determinant of the success of these operations. Two major developments affecting the economic base of the system will also affect agriculture. One, urbanization, is already underway, and is examined in Chapter Four. The second, energy development, is a strong possibility for the future, and is discussed in Chapter Five.

CHAPTER FOUR

URBANIZATION AND AGRICULTURE

Introduction

It is axiomatic that people have to live somewhere; in recent years that "somewhere" has been the Front Range of Colorado for a rapidly increasing number of people. This growth in population has focused on the so-called urban corridor connecting Fort Collins, Denver, Colorado Springs, and Pueblo. As that growth continues, it must inevitably place increasing pressure on the Running Creek Watershed, which runs parallel to and just east of this corridor of expansion. Metropolitan Denver's expansion toward the watershed is shown in Fig. 4.1.

The watershed, which is largely rural, thus faces demands to become increasingly urban. These demands pose difficult choices. As discussed in Chapter Three, the watershed is a resource now devoted primarily to the production of food. It contains substantial deposits of lignite coal, which may be needed to provide the fuel needed by increasing populations. But food production, energy development, and urbanization cannot occur in the same place at the same time; they may even make disagreeable neighbors.

The Growth Phenomenon*

The watershed is contained in four counties: Weld, Arapahoe, Adams and Elbert. Adams and Arapahoe are heavily urbanized and have experienced rapid growth. Weld is largely urbanized and has experienced somewhat slower growth; Elbert is rural and has experienced considerable growth only in recent years.

Table 4.1 tells the story explicitly. For Colorado, growth during the '60's has been largely an urban experience; the rural population was virtually stable over the decade. Adams and Arapahoe had declining rural populations and rapidly increasing urban ones. Almost all of Weld County's population increase was in its urban population. This pattern of increasing urbanization has, of course, been characteristic of the United States almost since its beginning.

Increasing population growth generates, and is generated by, increasing employment. A simple but useful descriptive device is to sort changing employment levels into three components of change. First, employment in a given sector in a region might simply increase with national employment. Second, local employment might change in a given sector as national employment in that sector changes relative to other sectors. This effect will be amplified or reduced as local concentration in that sector is greater than or less than national concentration in that sector. Finally, local employment might change because the area now produces a greater share of the nation's output.

Tables 4.2 to 4.5 show this categorization. The first two columns compare distribution of the work force for the U.S. with that of each county.

from left to right: Mary Anderson, Gayle Packard-Seeburger, H. Kenneth Gayer, Tim Tregarthen, Victor Hornbein

*These sections are based on Tregarthen, "Urbanizing Rural Land: Markets and Politics."

Fig. 4.1 Growth of the City and County of Denver, 1901-1974

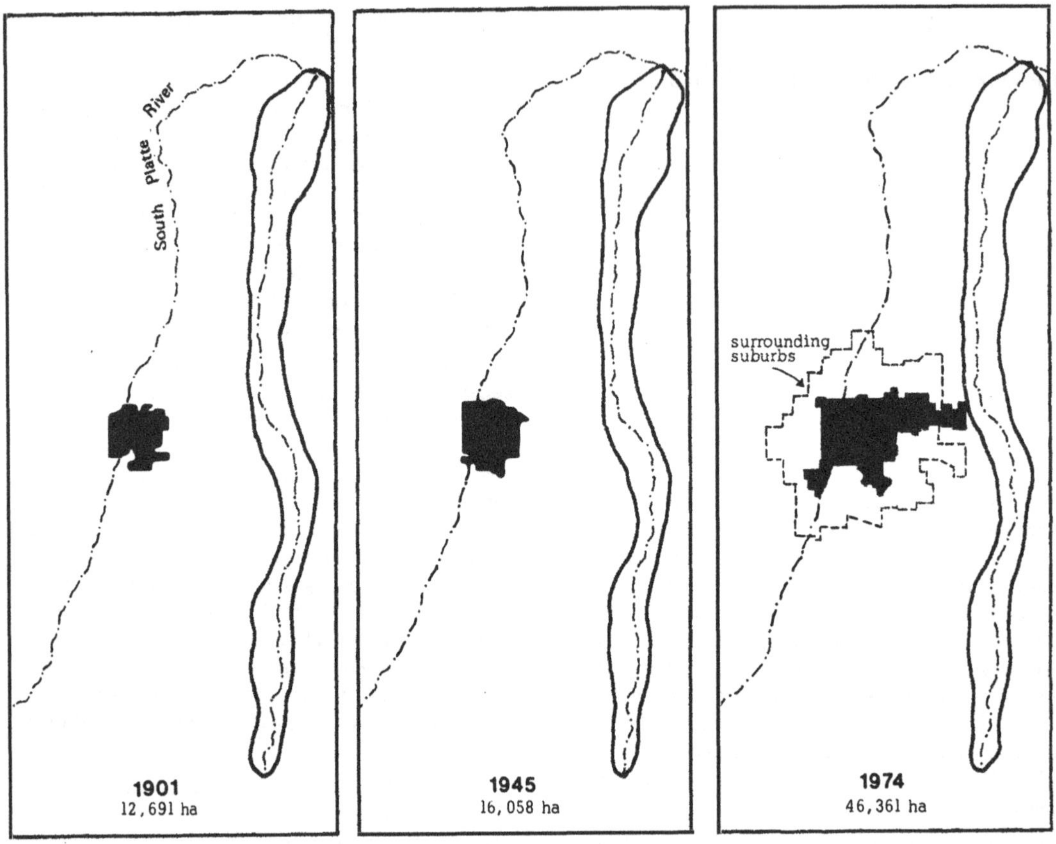

Table 4.1 Population Change 1960-1970 (numbers in thousands)

Unit	1960 Rural	1960 Urban	1960 Total	1970 Rural	1970 Urban	1970 Total	Percentage Change Rural	Percentage Change Urban	Percentage Change Total
Colorado	461.0	1,292.0	1,754.0	474.0	1,733.0	2,207.0	4.0	34.0	28.0
Adams	14.0	105.0	120.0	12.0	174.0	186.0	-17.0	64.0	54.0
Arapahoe	9.0	104.0	113.0	4.0	158.0	162.0	-67.0	52.0	43.0
Elbert	4.0	---	4.0	4.0	---	4.0	5.0	---	5.0
Weld	46.0	26.0	72.0	48.0	41.0	89.0	4.0	58.0	23.0

Table 4.2 Components of Employment Change — Adams County: 1960-1970

Industry	Percentage of 1960 U.S. Employment
Agriculture	12
Mining	1
Construction	5
Manfacturing	27
Trans., Pub. Utilities, Commerce	7
Wholesale, Retail Trade	18
Finance, Industry, Real Estate	4
Services	12
Government	14
TOTAL	

Table 4.3 Components of Employment Change — Arapahoe County: 1960-1970

Industry	Percentage of 1960 U.S. Employment
Agriculture	12
Mining	1
Construction	5
Manufacturing	27
Trans., Pub. Utilities, Commerce	7
Wholesale, Retail Trade	18
Finance, Industry, Real Estate	4
Services	12
Government	14
TOTAL	

EMPLOYMENT		COMPONENTS OF CHANGE		
Percentage of 1960 Adams Co. Employment	Percentage Increase in Adams Co. 1960-70	National Growth	Industry Mix	Local Shares
4	-3	23	-59	33
1	58	23	-35	70
10	36	23	-6	19
22	52	23	-8	37
12	56	23	-11	44
22	99	23	8	68
4	129	23	15	91
15	105	23	33	49
10	85	23	27	35
	73	23	4	46

EMPLOYMENT		COMPONENTS OF CHANGE		
Percentage of 1960 Arapahoe Co. Employment	Percentage Increase in Arapahoe Co. 1960-70	National Growth	Industry Mix	Local Shares
2	-21	23	-59	15
1	132	23	-35	144
8	23	23	-6	6
26	10	23	-8	-5
8	50	23	-11	38
20	94	23	8	63
5	115	23	15	77
19	92	23	33	36
10	98	23	27	48
	61	23	6	32

Table 4.4 Components of Employment Change — Elbert County: 1960-1970

Industry	Percentage of 1960 U.S. Employment
Agriculture	12
Mining	1
Construction	5
Manufacturing	27
Trans., Pub. Utilities, Commerce	7
Wholesale, Retail Trade	18
Finance, Industry, Real Estate	4
Services	12
Government	14
TOTAL	

Table 4.5 Components of Employment Change — Weld County: 1960-1970

Industry	Percentage of 1960 U.S. Employment
Agriculture	12
Mining	1
Construction	5
Manufacturing	27
Trans., Pub. Utilities, Commerce	7
Wholesale, Retail Trade	18
Finance, Industry, Real Estate	4
Services	12
Government	14
TOTAL	

EMPLOYMENT		COMPONENTS OF CHANGE		
Percentage of 1960 Elbert Co. Employment	Percentage Increase in Elbert Co. 1960-70	National Growth	Industry Mix	Local Shares
49	-15	23	-59	21
1	243	23	-35	255
9	9	23	-6	-8
5	76	23	-8	61
7	-43	23	-11	-55
12	22	23	-8	-9
2	0	23	14	-36
5	134	23	33	78
10	60	23	27	10
	11	23	-25	13

EMPLOYMENT		COMPONENTS OF CHANGE		
Percentage of 1960 Weld Co. Employment	Percentage Increase in Weld Co. 1960-1970	National Growth	Industry Mix	Local Shares
26	-23	23	-59	21
1	-32	23	-35	255
8	29	23	-6	-8
10	93	23	-8	61
7	10	23	-11	-55
18	52	23	-8	-9
4	85	23	14	36
15	60	23	33	78
12	73	23	27	10
	36	23	-25	13

John Stencel

Again, Adams, and Arapahoe show up as being largely urbanized, providing trade and services for the Denver area. Elbert and Weld are concentrated in agriculture, apparently importing manufactured goods.

The third column shows the percentage change in employment in each sector from 1960-1970. It is this percentage change that is to be distributed among the three factors described above. Note that agricultural employment declined during this period in each of the four counties.

U.S. employment increased by 23 percent during the decade; this is reported in the fourth column. The fifth column shows what the effect would have been if each sector had deviated in growth from the national average in the same way that national sectors did. Note that while this again yields identical entries for each county by sector, the total values are different. Because Elbert and Weld counties had high concentrations of employment in agriculture, which experienced decline nationally, total change due to industry mix shows a negative number.

The final column shows the remaining growth factor — increases due to increased local activity relative to the national pattern. All four counties showed an increase in agricultural employment rel ative to the rest of the nation; Adams County showed a relative increase in all employment sectors.

Future Prospects

The past is often an unreliable guide to the future. The population of the U.S. has in the last few years been playing Bicentennial tricks on demographers and planners. The urbanization trend noted above is showing signs of reversal; non-metropolitan counties have been growing faster than metropolitan ones since 1970. This reflects a shift to smaller cities from larger ones, however, not a shift to rural areas. Furthermore, the rate of population growth is declining generally, and the rate at which the population has been shifting westward has been declining. Households are getting smaller — and more numerous.

If this current trend toward relatively slower metropolitan growth continues, the rapid expansion in population and economic activity in Adams and Arapahoe may slow in the next twenty years. Weld and Elbert may, on the other hand, be in line for more rapid increases. Elbert County, in particular, would experience expansion as its population becomes large enough to support local service sectors, thus reducing its heavy dependence on imported goods and services. The watershed itself will come under even greater urbanization pressure than it has experienced in the past.

Increased pressure for urbanization on the watershed will be reflected in the market for land. Consumers will seek subdivision development of agricultural land, and will do so by offering prices that might tempt farmers and ranchers to sell. This is, of course, already happening at various points along the watershed. The problem of public policy is to determine whether the market is operating efficiently in providing incentives for the conversion of agricultural land.

Consider the urbanization problem. If people want to live in the rural environment of the watershed and offer to pay for that then they will send signals to farmers and ranchers, via the price system, of their interest. Suppose that a rancher is earning a net return of $80 per hectare per year. The price system is in effect sending the rancher a message stating that the net value of having the rancher using that land to produce beef is $80 annually, a sum equivalent to having $1000 earning eight percent interest. A bid of $1500 per hectare for the same land for urban development will reflect the market's price signal as to the benefits to society of using the resources for the production of shelter rather than food.

The rancher is now faced with information necessary for a decision on the use of land. Suppose he or she expects the $80 return to continue indefinitely, and that no increase in the offer price of developers is expected. If the rancher sells, the $1500 could be set aside at eight percent interest to earn $120 per year; this is in effect the annual per hectare cost of staying in ranching (note that this example ignores tax considerations). The rancher, absent any particular preference for a life of struggling with land and nature, will sell. The problem, again, is to determine whether he or she is responding to the correct set of signals as given by the market.

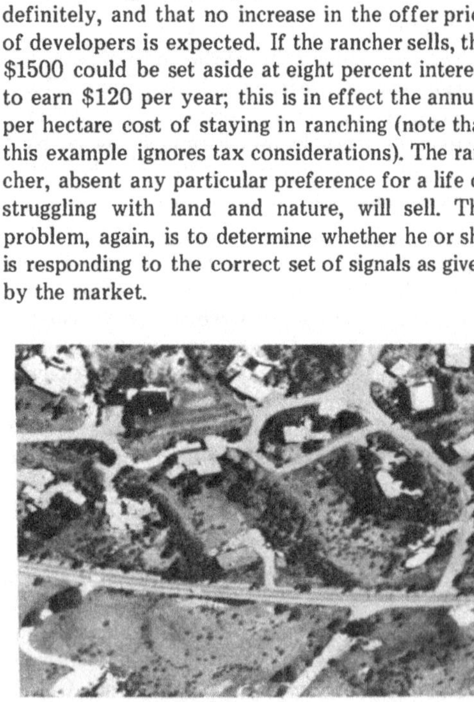

A Subdivision

The Externality Problem

In economics, as in ecology, everything is thought to affect everything else. A correct answer to the question, "What does that have to do with the price of tea in China?" is, "something." As noted above, the role of the price system is to reflect these effects so that decision makers are faced with the costs and benefits of their decisions. There are a number of reasons, however, that the market will not achieve this goal in allocating watershed land.

Consider again the rancher's decision problem described above. The benefits of staying in ranching are reflected by the present *and expected future* prices of food (the market does create an incentive to consider the needs of future generations — at least for food). But society may receive additional benefits from watershed ranching operations — benefits not reflected in the price signals facing the rancher.

Agricultural operations provide open space. This space may yield aesthetic benefits for neighboring urban dwellers. It aids in flood control, thus benefitting downstream property owners. Open space also aids in reducing air pollution. These benefits are real, but the market reflects none of them. Many individuals, no doubt, greatly appreciate open land on the watershed; it is unlikely that any of them have ever paid a rancher or farmer anything for this service. An individual will get the same benefit regardless of whether he or she pays for it; it is therefore tempting not to pay. The same is not true of food; one must pay for that commodity to get it. Thus the market sends signals reflecting the value of food production but not of open space. The urbanization process operates with a deck stacked in its favor — with excessive urbanization the result of unregulated market choices.

A different set of externality problems emerges from some types of conflict between ranchers and farmers on their own land and subdivision developments on the other. First, agricultural operations require the movement of machinery from field to field. Scattered subdivision development may impede easy movement of this sort; slow moving farm equipment may in turn be regarded as a nuisance by commuters in a hurry to get to work on time.

Other common agricultural practices — application of fertilizers, pesticides, and herbicides — that were once unobjectionable may take on a different character in the context of neighboring residential development. As this development increases, pressure on agricultural operators to revise their practices may increase. This revision is likely, in general, to increase the cost of such operations, and thus increase the flow of agricultural land to other uses.

Crops & Pastureland

More generally, increased residential development inevitably changes the character of a rural community. If this initial character is viewed by ranchers and farmers as contributing to their quality of life, then that factor must be counted in the "real" profits discussed in Chapter Three. Residential development might thus reduce these profits, again increasing the flow of agricultural land to other uses. "Rural character" can thus be regarded as an economic good; whether ranchers and farmers own property rights to rural character is discussed in Chapter Six.

There are additional effects on urbanization on agriculture that *are* reflected in the market. These "pecuniary" externalities occur when changing demands from one sector affect the operation of another. These do not create the kinds of efficiency problems that appear in the cases cited above, but it is useful to note them in examining the impact of urbanization:

1. Urbanization processes increase uncertainty in the market for land. Farmers unsure about the pace of urban development will be reluctant to invest in fixed capital assets such as barns and silos which may eventually reduce the value of the land for urbanization.
2. As agricultural operations are shut down in the face of urbanization, support services for these operations will begin to leave as well. These developments will increase the costs of agricultural operations.
3. The fragmentation of land ownership that comes with urbanization, together with physical development itself, makes the development decision a difficult one to reverse. Present development eliminates options that would otherwise have been available in the future.
4. As urban settlements increase in population, the demand for residential water will increase. These users may be able to out-bid agricultural users of water altogether; in any event, they will increase its price. Operators of irrigated farms in the northern end of the watershed already face the prospect of losing their irrigation water to the cities of Thornton and Westminster.

James R. Miller

Curtiss E. Frank

Urbanization and the Public Sector*

The development process will, of course, create increased demands for public services. This would create no particular difficulty in a world in which individuals were charged correctly for the services they consumed, but this is unlikely to be the case.

Urban development is likely to create a need for increased personal services from the public sector. Such services tend to increase the per capita cost of government services; as new residents push these per capita costs up, all residents bear the burden. Average cost taxing in the face of increasing per capita costs constitutes a subsidy for new residents paid by existing ones.

A further difficulty posed by the urbanization of rural land is that it is likely to increase the degree of heterogeneity of individual preferences. This diversity of views will make it more difficult for local governments to devise policies satisfactory to most citizens. In general, if citizens in a jurisdiction have similar preferences with respect to public sector services, then the public sector will be more efficient in meeting these needs. If widely differing views exist within a jurisdiction, efficiency will be reduced. Increased urbanization would, of course, reduce the heterogeneity of preferences in counties that are now largely urbanized, such as Arapahoe and Adams.

With the exception of this problem of increased heterogeneity of preferences, the economic burdens of increasing growth can in principle be priced so as to place these costs on the new residents that generate them. The attempt to do so is not simply a matter of equity; it is necessary if decision-makers are to be faced with the full costs and benefits of their decisions. This suggests that common objections to increased growth — such as the argument that an area does not have enough schools for new citizens — really involve institutional problems in the tax system. This was illustrated just prior to the conference when a proposal for a school tax increase in western Elbert County necessitated by growth in the Elizabeth area was rejected by school district voters.

Eric Walther, William Lord

*This section based on William B. Lord, "Decision Making for Food Production," and Timothy D. Tregarthen, "Urbanizing Rural Land: Markets and Politics," papers prepared for the Food, Fuel, and Shelter Conference.

Agricultural-Urban Conversions

Many of the factors examined in the discussion to this point can now be summarized in the descriptive model outlined in Chapter One. Table 4.6 lists factors that might affect changes in land use within the agricultural categories already discussed, changes from agricultural uses to urban uses, and from lower to higher densities.

The environmental factors listed include precipitation, length of growing season, wildlife pest controls (e.g. the lark bunting as an aid to control of grasshoppers), and location (proximity to urban areas). The economic demand factor is listed as food prices. Supply factors affecting costs of agricultural operations include land prices, water prices, energy prices, environmental controls (limits on burning, pesticides, etc.), and other operating costs.

The political and social factors listed include taxes and the segment of the community that dominates decisions — whether decisions are dominated by rural values or by suburban values. The absence of an entry in a particular cell suggests that there is no strong effect; plus and minus signs indicate that the factor increases or decreases the rate of the land use change involved.

Note that high density development is assumed here to economize on energy, water, and the cost of public services. It is thus encouraged by higher prices for each of these.

As noted in Chapter One, changes in land use can, in turn, affect a factor. Factor-change relationships can thus be mutually reinforcing. These patterns can work through a variety of channels. For example, increased land prices resulting from residential demands would increase the flow of land out of agriculture, increasing operating costs of remaining agricultural operations. Table 4.7 lists the same changes and factors that appeared in Table 4.6; changes in land use are now shown as affecting factors. Note that some factors, such as food prices, are not affected by events within the watershed system.

The causal relations listed here are speculative results of conference discussions. Further research may reveal errors; it will certainly identify other factors that determine and are affected by agricultural-urban land use changes. The important thing is to begin to identify what affects what — and how?

Food and shelter relationships have now been described. Chapter Five examines fuel development. The political system's response to all of this and some of the value considerations that form the basis for those responses will be assessed in Chapter Six.

Eli Yakich, Jr.

Table 4.6 Factors in Agricultural-Urban Changes in Land Use

FACTORS / FLOWS	Precipitation	Growing Season	Pest/ Predators	Location	Food Prices	Land Prices	Water Prices	Energy Prices	Environmental Controls	Operating Costs	Taxes	Rural Domination	Suburban Domination
Irrigation to Dryland	+						+						
Irrigation to Pasture	+					-	+	+	+				
Irrigation to Low Density		-	-	+	-	+	+		+	+	+	-	+
Irrigation to Med. Density		-	-	+	-	+	+		+	+	+	-	+
Irrigation to High Density		-	-	+	-	+	+	+	+	+	+	-	-
Dryland to Irrigation	-						-						
Dryland to Pasture						-		+	+				
Dryland to Low Density	-	-	-	+	-	+			+	+	+	-	+
Dryland to Med. Density	-	-	-	+	-	+			+	+	+	-	+
Dryland to High Density	-	-	-	+	-	+		+	+	+	+	-	-
Pasture to Irrigation	-					+	-	-	-				
Pasture to Dryland						+		-	-				
Pasture to Low Density	-	-	-	+	-	+		-		+	+	-	+
Pasture to Med. Density	-	-	-	+	-	+		-		+	+	-	+
Pasture to High Density	-	-	-	+	-	+				+	+	-	-
Low Density to Medium Density				+		+		+			-	-	+
Low Density to High Density				+		+	+	+			+	-	-
Med. Density to High Density				+		+	+	+			+	-	-

Table 4.7 Effects of Agricultural-Urban Land Use Changes on Factors

Suburban Domination	Rural Domination	Taxes	Operating Costs	Environmental Controls	Energy Prices	Water Prices	Land Prices	Food Prices	Location	Pest/Predators	Growing Season	Precipation	FACTORS / FLOWS
		-	-		-	-	-						Irrigation to Dry Land
	-	-	-		-	-	-			-	-		Irrigation to Pasture
+	+	+	+	+	+	+	+		+				Irrigation to Low Density
+	-	+	+	+	+	+	+		+				Irrigation to Med. Density
	-	+	+	+	+	+	+		+				Irrigation to High Density
		+	+		+	+	+						Dryland to Irrigation
													Dryland to Pasture
+	+	+	+	+	+	+	+		+	-	-		Dryland to Low Density
+	-	+	+	+	+	+	+		+	-	-		Dryland to Med. Density
	-	+	+	+	+	+	+		+	-	-		Dryland to High Density
		+	+		+	+	+				+		Pasture to Irrigation
		+	+		+		+				+		Pasture to Dryland
+	+	+	+	+	+	+	+		+	-	-		Pasture to Low Density
+	-	+	+	+	+	+	+		+	-	-		Pasture to Med. Density
-	-	+	+	+	+	+	+		+	-	-		Pasture to High Density
+	-	+	+	+	+	+	+		+	-			Low Density to Med. Density
-	-	+	+	+	+	+	+		+	-			Low Density to High Density
-	-	+	+	+	+	+	+		+	-	-		Med. Density to High Density

CHAPTER FIVE

PROSPECTIVE WATERSHED ENERGY DEVELOPMENT

Energy Demand and the Watershed*

Whether one prefers to regard the finite nature of fossil fuels as a crisis, problem, or challenge, the impact of the inevitably increasing scarcity of these fuels will be widely felt. The result of this scarcity is already appearing in the form of higher energy prices; their impact on watershed agriculture and possible urbanization has been discussed above. It is the watershed's own energy resources that are of concern in this chapter — their development would have a substantial effect on the system.

While uranium and other minerals exist in the watershed, the primary resource of interest in this area, as well as much of the interior west, is coal. Figure 5.1 shows projections by the Colorado Energy Research Institute of energy consumption by source in the U.S. through the year 2000. The dominant role of coal in the forecast is clear.

Coal also plays a critical role in national energy planning. While its role in the U.S. has been shrinking — to a contribution of less than one-fifth of the energy used today from a level of nearly one-half after World War II — there is evidence that that process is reversing. Coal is increasingly what the U.S. has left by way of energy; it now comprises approximately 80 percent of domestic energy reserves. Coal is already a major factor in the production of electricity, providing 46 percent of electricity generated. Many regions, including Colorado, are already using all of their hydroelectric capacities. The U.S. Congress has proscribed the construction of new electrical generating plants based on oil and gas, and is encouraging existing plants which use these fuels to convert to coal. Finally, the energy program proposed by President Carter in the Spring of 1977 places heavy emphasis on the increased use of coal.

David Ver Steeg

This chapter is based in part on D.H. Hebb, A.K. Turner, and D.J. Ver Steeg, "The Energy Dilemma," prepared for the conference, and, Cameron Engineers, Inc., "The Watkins Project," Denver: April, 1975

Fig. 5.1 United States Energy Consumption by Source, 1974-2000

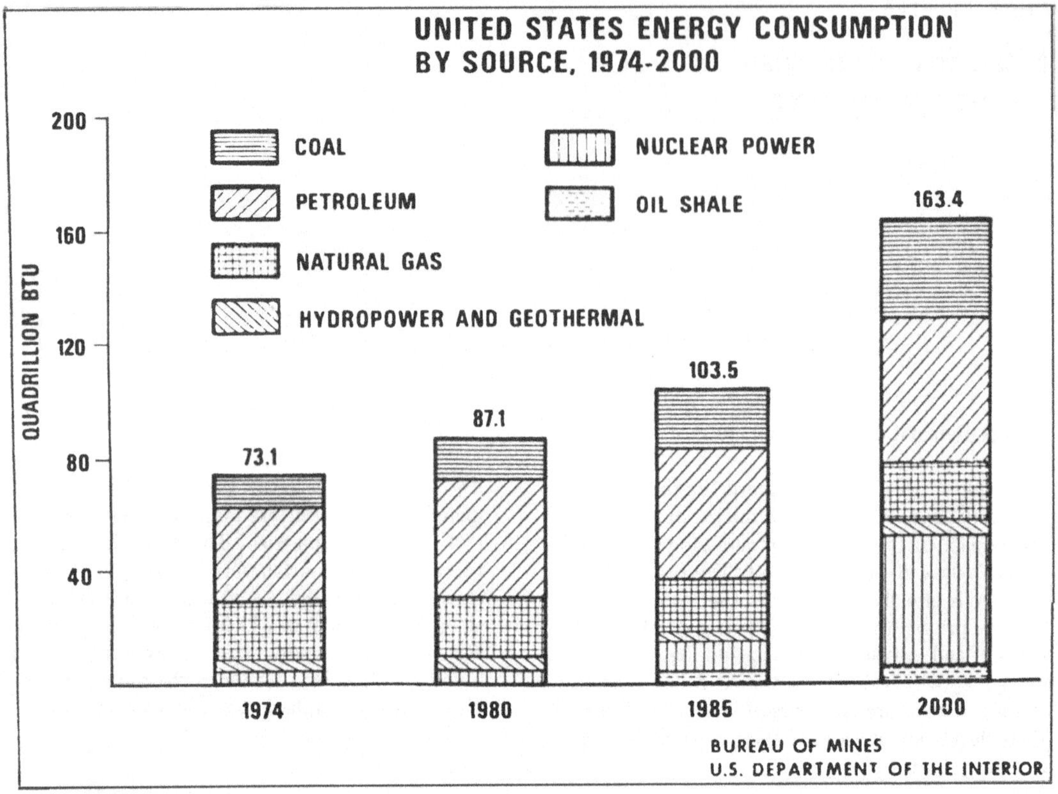

Solar energy seems to offer a tempting panacea to energy problems. Estimates of its costs relative to other energy sources vary widely. It is a new industry; its further development may begin to close whatever gap in cost now exists. As a new industry, it faces the difficulties of inadequate support activities as well as cost. Bank financing for domestic installations, building codes, and the lack of a service industry to provide for the maintenance of solar systems are among the factors impeding its development.

But the factor of primary relevance to coal development on the watershed is the rapidly increasing cost of natural gas. The shortages that these price increases reflect must worsen; serious shortages of natural gas in Colorado are expected as early as the late 1970's. It happens that the coal underlying the watershed is well-suited for gasification; it is this role that seems most likely for it.

Denver Basin Coals

Coal deposits that form what is known as the Denver Basin are mapped in Figure 5.7. These coals began forming in the Paleocene age, and lie above the extensively mined coals of the Laramie formation. This zone of coal is more than 150 meters thick in some places. The area of deposits that are within about 300 meters of the earth's surface is about 50 kilometers wide and 125 kilometers long, stretching from a point just northeast of Denver to a point a few miles south of Calhan. As much as 18 billion metric tons of coal may lie in this area.

The rating of most of this coal is lignite *A* (based on standards of the American Society for Testing and Materials); some of the coal is graded as high as sub-bituminous *C*. These are low quality coals in terms of their ability to generage heat. They are, however, low in sulfur content — a factor that is advantageous in terms of air pollution problems.

Fig. 5.2 Mineral and geologic resources of the Watershed

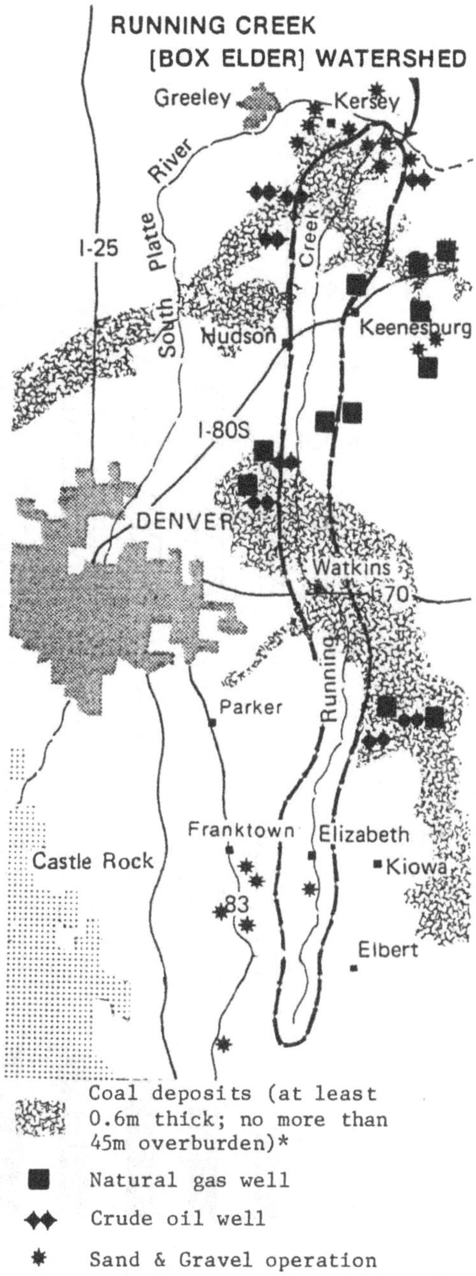

* from Speltz, C.N. Strippable Coal Resources of Colorado PR 195, US Bureau of Mines, 1974

Comparison of Heat Values and Proximate Analyses (Moist, Ash-free Basis) of Coal of Different Ranks

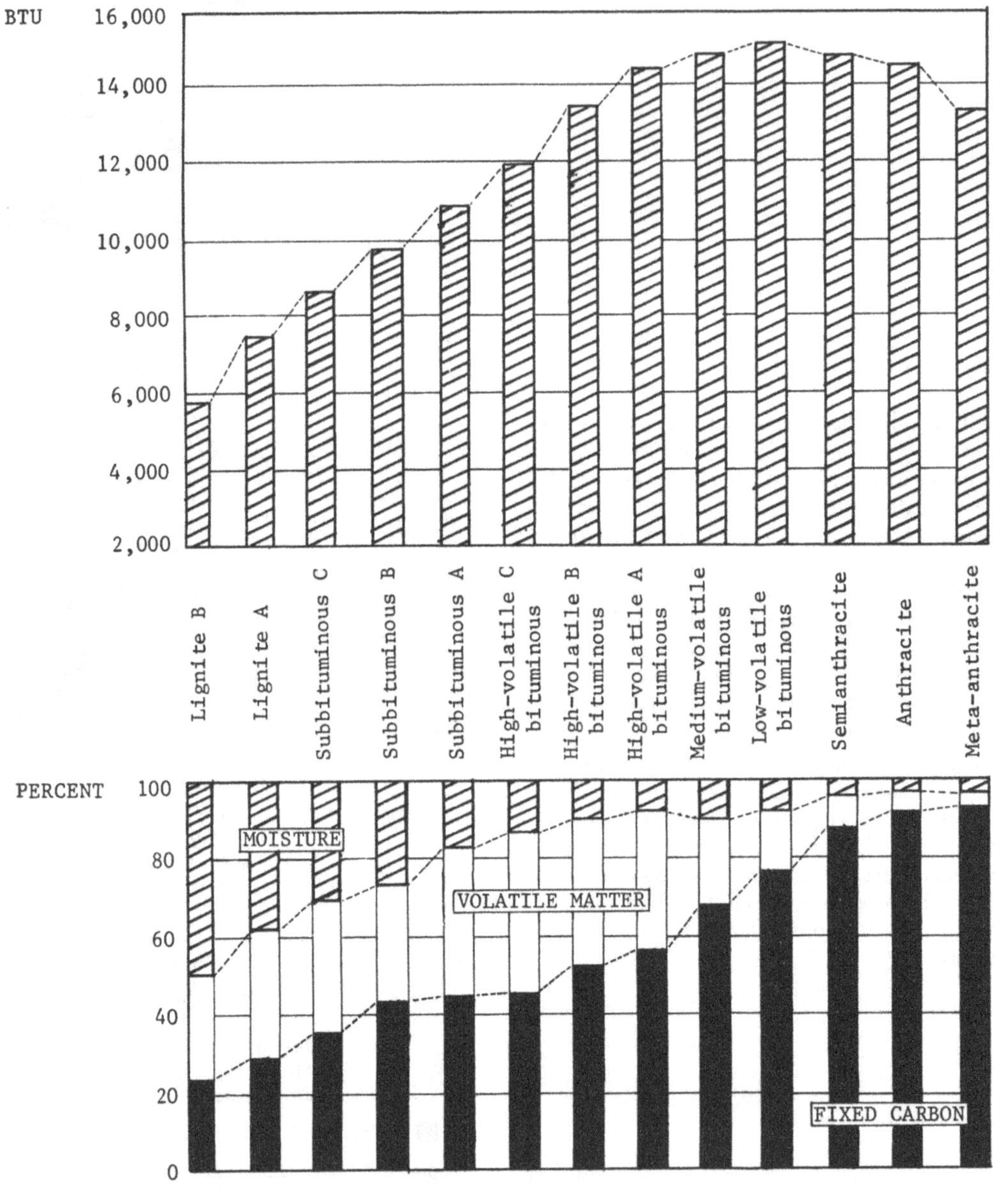

(from: Averitt, Paul, USGS, *Geologic Atlas of the Rocky Mountain Region*, RMAG, 1972, p. 297)

The Watkins Project

Particular interest in the Denver Basin has centered in the Watkins area. More than 200 exploratory holes were drilled in the area in 1965 by the Public Service Company of Colorado and by private geologists. This drilling suggested the existence of thick lignite beds at relatively shallow depths. Subsequent exploration by Cameron Engineers, Inc., a Colorado firm, confirmed these findings. Cameron Engineers is project manager for Mintech Corporation and Marathon Oil Company, which jointly own mineral lease interests in the area. Cameron has developed a proposal for the gasification of this resource; this project has been projected to produce more than seven million cubic meters per day of pipeline quality synthetic gas; i.e. a substitute for natural gas. This quantity would be sufficient to satisfy about 40 percent of the present demand for natural gas from the Denver area.

The area suggested by Cameron for what has come to be known as the Watkins Project covers about 3000 hectares, and contains more than 304 million metric tons of recoverable lignite in a seam that averages 7.6 meters in thickness and lies an average 27 meters beneath the surface; the depth ranges from 6 to 57 meters.

This lignite would be mined over a period of 27 years, with about 11.3 million metric tons removed each year. Mining would begin on the east side of Running Creek, near Watkins, and proceed westerly. Surface cuts would be 38 meters wide, and about 2130 meters in length during the first five years of the project. These cuts would double in length for the next five years of the project, and would decrease in length after that.

The proposal calls for reclamation of the soil, with the surface graded to approximate its original contour. Reclamation efforts are expected to follow within two or three cuts of the working pit; major reclamation activities would be undertaken within an 18 month period after the mining of any one cut was completed. The top meter of soil removed in the initial cut would be retained and used as topsoil for the reclaimed surface. Whether reclamation can be completed in a short time in the semi-arid environment of the watershed remains a subject of debate.

The gasification process itself involves heating the coal with steam, increasing its available hydrogen so that the hydrogen reacts with carbon in the coal to form the methane gas synthetic fuel. The heat to generate the steam would be provided by burning some of the coal from the mine, as well as burning solid wastes and sewage sludge from the Denver metropolitan area. Ashes separated in the coal during the gasification process would be buried in the mine, as would non-combustible wastes from the Denver area.

Kenneth D'Appolonia, Catherine Ingraham

Table 5.1 Types and Sources of Potential Air Pollutants from Coal Conversion Processes [1]

Pollutant	Process-Generated	Combustion-Generated
Particulate Matter	x	x
Sulfur Oxides	x	x
Reduced Sulfur Compounds	x	
Nitrogen Oxides		x
Hydrocarbons		x
Carbon Monoxide	x	x
Trace Metals	x	x
Odors	x	
Other Gases (including NH_3, HCN, NCl)	x	

[1] E.S. Rubin and F.C. McMichael, "Some Implications of Environmental Regulatory Activities on Coal Conversion Processes," Presented at the EPA Symposium on Environmental Aspects of Fuel Conversion Technology, May 13-16, 1974, St. Louis, Missouri.
Cameron Engineers, Inc., "The Watkins Project", Denver: April, 1975.

In addition to the synthetic gas produced, there are a number of other by-products of the gasification process. Liquid hydrocarbons would be produced at a rate of about 425,000 metric tons per year. Some of these would be sold as specialty chemical feedstocks, some would be hydrogenated to produce motor fuel, and the remainder would be gasified to produce added project gas. 145,800 metric tons of aqueous ammonia would be produced annually. Some of this would be used to fertilize the reclaimed mine for revegetation; the remainder would be sold to farmers. Pelletized sulfur — 36,900 metric tons annually — would be exported to phosphate rock plants in Utah, Idaho, and Wyoming; some would also be used in fertilizers. A layer of kaolinite occurs with the lignite coal in the area. This would emerge as ash in the gasification process. This calcined kaolinitic ash, some 3.78 million metric tons annually, would be used in building bricks, concrete aggregates, and road surfacing.

Air pollution would also be a by-product of this coal gasification activity. Table 5.1 lists the types and sources of potential air pollutants. Watkins is outside the Denver airshed. More study would be required to determine the effects of these potential pollutants on other areas and in the Watkins area itself.

In addition to the location of the coal itself, a number of factors contribute to the potential viability of the Watkins site. As noted in Chapter One, it is unusual in its provision of a major energy deposit adjacent to a major metropolitan area. This is important not only as a factor in the demand for gas to be produced, but in supply considerations as well. Proximity to Denver provides a ready labor pool and a wide range of services to a large industrial operation.

A variety of transportation services are available. Figure 5.3 shows that proposed service of the Denver Regional Transportation District will provide access to the project site. As shown in Figure 5.3, the site has ready highway and rail access, and is close to Stapleton International Airport. Existing Colorado Interstate Gas Company pipelines would be sufficient to carry gas to the market; these pipelines converge less than two kilometers southwest of the site. While the mine may be self-sufficient in providing energy for its operations, additional power could be purchased from Public Service; a transmission line crosses the site.

Water for the project would come from treated and waste water from Denver. The project would require 10.5 million kiloliters of waste water per year, an amount which Cameron engineers regarded as readily available. The water would be used for steam generation, cooling, and dust control in the mining operations. Cameron projections indicate that none of it would be returned to streams or aquifers.

It is not certain at this point when, if ever, the Watkins project will proceed. The project exists now as a proposal. If federal subsidies for coal gasification projects become available, the project would probably proceed immediately, meaning that the plant would be operative by about 1980. A lack of federal funds would delay the project, but it seem inevitable that, unless alternative energy sources become available at low costs, rising natural gas prices will make the project profitable in the future.

The mine has been estimated to have a total cost of $96 million, including restoration to original contours, restoration of the topsoil, and reseeding. These reclamation costs represent approximately one-quarter of this estimated cost. The plant has an estimated cost of $524 million. (These 1973 estimates have been converted to 1976 dollars). To earn a 15 percent return on this investment, gas produced would have to sell for six to eight cents per cubic meter. The City of Colorado Springs now pays an average of about three cents per cubic meter. Natural gas prices would thus need to double relative to other prices before the plant could become profitable by the Cameron estimates.

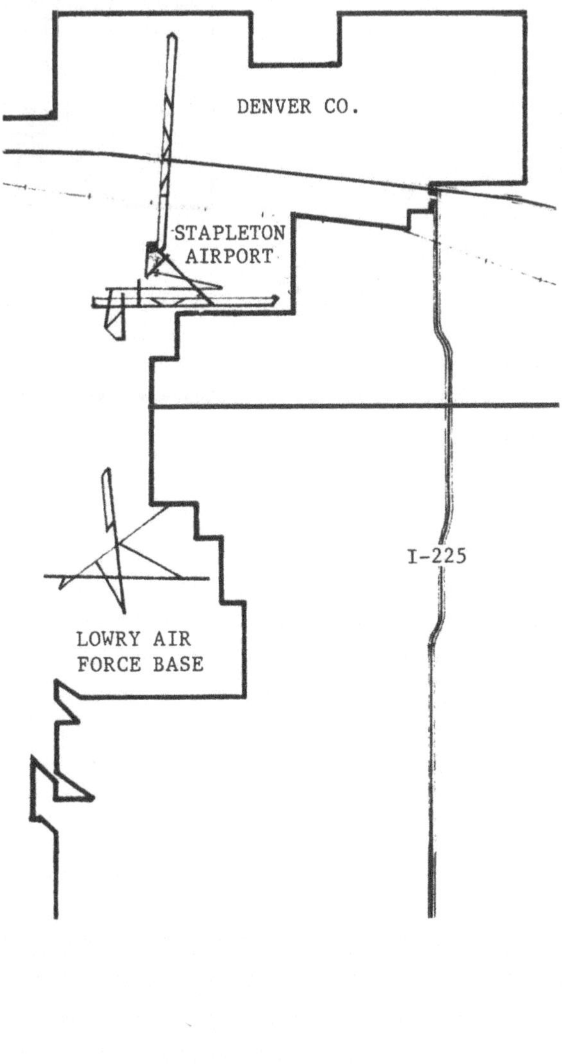

Fig. 5.3 Watkins Project Transportation Access

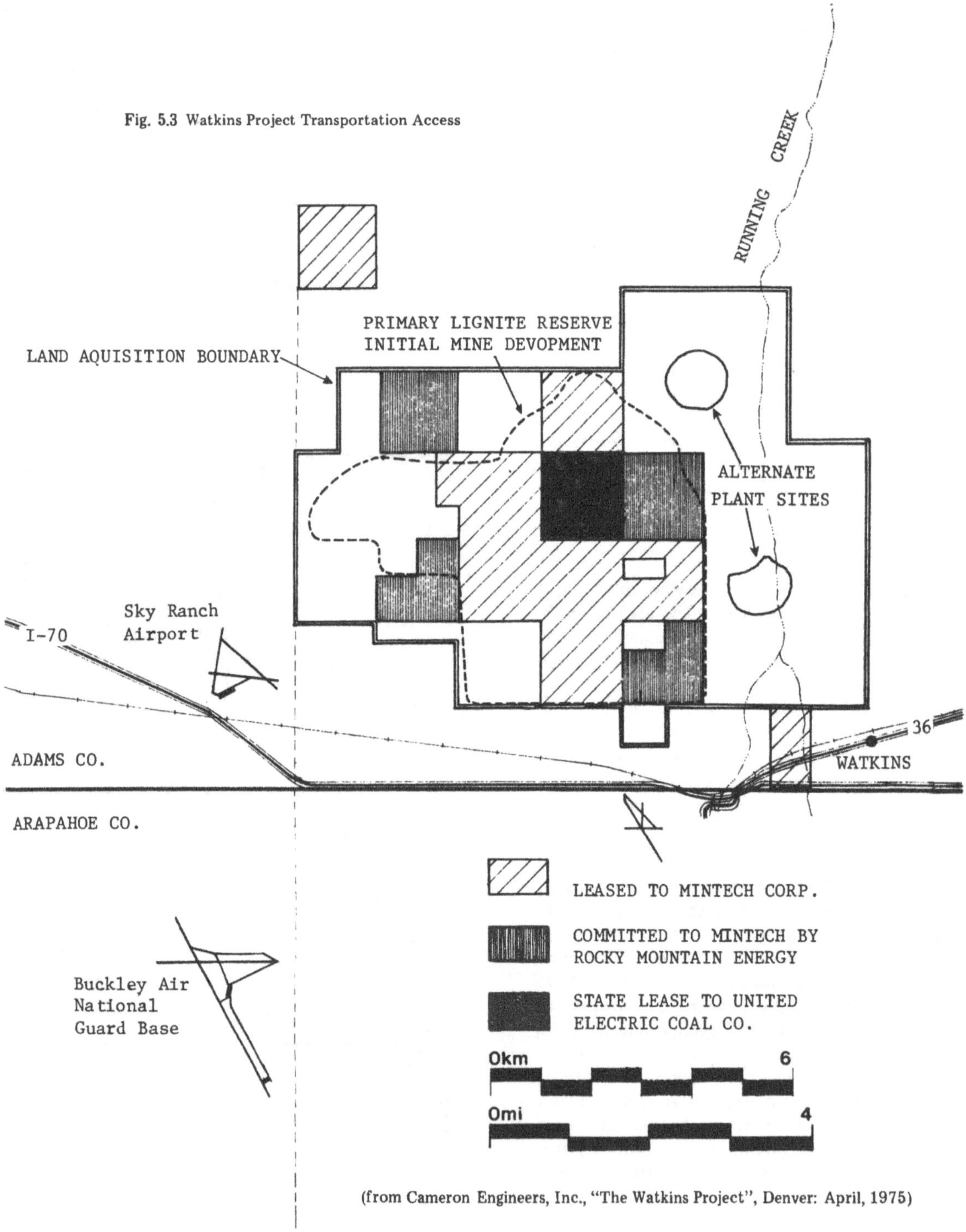

(from Cameron Engineers, Inc., "The Watkins Project", Denver: April, 1975)

The Watkins Project and Land Use Changes

If the Watkins Project is developed, it will have a major impact on the watershed. Cameron Engineers has estimated that it would employ 937 people annually during the 27 year projected life of the mine. Based on the number of added local jobs this would generate (see Chapter Three), the operation would attract a total population approaching that now on the watershed. Not all of these people would live on the watershed, of course, but the effect on the region would be substantial nonetheless.

The factors that will encourage the shift from agricultural land uses to surface mining — and back — are indicated in Table 5.2. Increased precipitation would increase agricultural profitability; this could slow conversion to coal development, although this effect is unlikely to be of great importance. Increased precipitation would also ease reclamation from coal to agriculture. It is assumed here that reclamation would be required; "regulatory difficulties" refers not to effective regulation but to possible unnecessary delay and expense that could be created by an inefficient regulatory process. Using the coal today would eliminate it as an option for the future; increasing concern for the rights of future generations relative to present generations would thus slow development, assuming that this concern were effectively expressed through the political system.

These factors, with the exceptions of land prices, regulatory difficulties, and concern for the future, are essentially exogenous to the local system. Changes in land use in and out of coal development would not effect them. The prospect of coal development should increase land prices, and force regulatory agencies to become more efficient (this latter effect is rather uncertain). It is unclear whether and how coal mining would influence local concern for the future.

Donald Crane

Table 5.2 Factor Effects on Coal Conversion

Coal to High Density	Coal to Med. Density	Coal to Low Density	Coal to Pasture	Coal to Dryland	Coal to Irrigation	Low Density to Coal	Pasture to Coal	Dryland to Coal	Irrigation to Coal	FLOWS / FACTORS
			+	+	+		-	-	-	Precipitation
-	-	-	-	-	-	+	+	+	+	Coal Quality and Access
+	+		+	+	+	+	+	+	+	Smooth Topography
						+	+	+	+	Mean Winter Temperature
						+	+	+	+	Price of Gas
						+	+	+	+	Prices of Gas By-Products
			+	+	+		-	-	-	Food Prices
-	-	-	-	-	-		-	-	-	Labor Costs
						-	-	-	-	Capital Costs
+	+					+	+	+	+	Land Prices
+	-					-	-	-	-	Transportation Costs
		-				-	-	-	-	Regulatory Difficulties
-		+	+	+	+	-	-	-	-	Future Generation Concerns

CHAPTER SIX

THE POLITICAL SYSTEM AND HUMAN VALUES

Land Use Policy in Colorado*

Conditions of the watershed's natural system, together with the supply and demand factors of the economic system, have combined historically to yield the present mix of land use on the watershed, a mix clearly dominated by agriculture. That mix is changing. Continuing urbanization pressures, together with prospective energy development, will cause land prices in the watershed to rise, making agriculture — a land intensive activity — less and less profitable as a land use alternative. As noted in Chapter Four, however, the marketplace is unlikely to reflect all of the costs and benefits of the land uses under consideration here; it may therefore provide decision-makers with incorrect information, resulting in a misallocation of land. This sort of misallocation, if it is to be corrected, will require intervention from the political system. This chapter examines the operation of that system and the human values it seeks to reflect.

Land use authority in Colorado is exercised largely by local governments. While their authority is essentially that delegated by the State, that delegation has been a broad one in the land use area. This delegation of authority to local governments has recently come under challenge, with the assertion that the state should play a stronger role. The state does not now deal with "land use" as such; it is responsible instead for specific factors relevant to it. These include water and air quality, subdivision development, energy needs, and recreation. This fragmentation of concerns is more than matched by a fragmentation of authority. State agencies with land use responsibilities include the Division of Planning, Land Use Commission, Office of the Environmental Coordinator in the Governor's office, Geological Survey, Water Conservation Board, Division of Water Resources, Water Quality Control Division, Groundwater Commission, Board of Land Commissioners, Air Pollution Control Commission, Solid Waste Disposal Program, Oil and Gas Conservation Commission, Division of Mines, Soil Conservation Board, State Forest Service, and the Highway Department. This bewildering array of 16 agencies has led inevitably to confusion about what state policy is. Such an array can only slow response to proposals. There does not exist a single agency with over-all land use authority over the others. If the state is to play an active role in land use policy, the creation of such an agency at high level, perhaps in the Governor's office, may be needed.

With the state unable to play an effective role, local governments are left with the major responsibilities. This is perhaps best illustrated in the energy field. Relevant federal policies are expressed in the Mineral Leasing Act of 1920, the National Environmental Policy Act of 1969, the Mining and Mineral Policy Act of 1970, and the Energy Policy and Conservation Act of 1975. The

*Much of the material in this section is based on Alan Merson, "Energy Development in the Watershed: Who Decides?" paper prepared for the Food, Fuel, and Shelter Conference, and on a conference address by Philip Savage, "Land Use Policy in Colorado."

dominant theme of the 1920 legislation was one of giving states the major role in mining and reclamation policy; this theme is continued under the more recent legislation.

Colorado, for its part, has recently amended and strengthened its Open Mining Land Reclamation Act, which provides for a Land Reclamation Board to issue permits for the surface mining of coal and other minerals. This Board is required to defer to local authority in reaching decisions.

Other state legislation strengthens the dominant local role in energy, and land use policy as well. House Bill 1041 mandates the identification, designation, and administration of mineral resource areas as matter of state interest, and requires counties and cities — not a state agency — to perform this task. Similarly, House Bill 1529 authorizes and requires counties to develop master plans for the development of mineral extraction within their jurisdictions. House Bill 1034 confirms in local governments the authority to take the broadest possible view of their authority to control growth within their jurisdictions in a way that best provides for local interests. Senate Bill 35 requires all counties to adopt subdivision regulations and to set minimum standards for subdividing land.

In short, the state has, through legislation and its own inadequacy, put the major responsibility for land use policy in the hands of local governments.

Two possible exceptions to this general thrust exist within the State Department of Health. This department has the responsibility under federal legislation — the 1970 Clean Air Amendment and the Federal Water Pollution Control Act (1972) — of meeting national air and water quality standards. The two commissions designated within the Department — the Air Pollution Control Commission and the Water Pollution Control Commission — have substantial potential power in land use. Land uses, whether subdivision developments or strip mining, clearly affect air and water quality. The federally mandated authority of these two commissions may well put the state in the land use regulatory business.

Alan Merson

Issues in Jurisdictional Authority

Two major and conflicting principles serve as guides to the delegation of land use authority by jurisdictions. One is that the jurisdiction making the decision encompass the effects of that decision. Otherwise, one jurisdiction can make choices which will have an impact on another, but with no political accountability for this impact. This principle, given the wide-ranging effects of many land use decisions, suggests increasing authority at the regional, state, and even federal levels. Further support of this argument is given by the lack of technical expertise that may exist at the local level.

But as jurisdictions grow larger, they encompass an increasingly diverse set of interests and values. Smaller jurisdictions may better reflect local interests, and offer more and easier access to government by constituents. Further, local governments are likely to be less specialized in function, and may thus confront a wider range of interests than do state or federal agencies with specific functional tasks. A Board of County Commissioners, while taking a more narrow geographical view, may have a broader view in terms of issues than an Air Pollution Control Commission or Bureau of Mines. This argues, of course, for the concentration of authority at local level.

The setting of jurisdictional limits of authority, like the decisions to which these limits will lead, thus involves trade-offs. The observation that a policy decision by the town of Elizabeth will affect the entire watershed does not imply that the watershed be organized as a regional government. Nor does the possibility that local governments better serve constituent interest imply that the state should have no role in land use planning.

Defining a "correct" division of power is probably not possible. In any event, the present delegation of land use authority is a long-standing one. Interjurisdictional conflict can be resolved at least in part by consultation and bargaining among jurisdictions. The state, for its part, could seek to play a unifying role in all of this. This would require restructuring of existing state authority to avoid the fragmentation of authority and responsibility that now exists.

Dwight Whitney

Property Rights for Rural Character?*

The primary effect of growth identified in Chapter Four was change in the nature of the community. A rural society is different from an urban one. Land use policy, responsibility for which resides at the local level, strongly influences this growth. The question emerges, then, as to whether local communities have a legitimate right to preserve their character, remembering that such preservation may require policies that exclude others from settling in them.

While the general legal answer to this question is still being developed, a fairly clear answer for much of the watershed already exists. Figure 6.1 shows areas on the watershed that are zoned for agricultural use. While the limitations implied by such zoning vary by county, development in such areas is typically proscribed.

This agricultural zoning effectively means that the respective jurisdictions imposing it own development rights to land thus zoned — such rights are clearly not owned by the landowners involved. Watershed counties could preserve the present agricultural character of the area simply by not granting the changes in zoning necessary for development.

But changing character and the development that induces it are not necessarily "bad"; they are simply changes involving costs and benefits. If the benefits of a change exceed the costs, then it should be made. In making such change, however, counties need not simply give away development rights by rezoning. These development rights are valuable assets owned by the county by virtue of its zoning authority. There is no conceptual reason charges could not be levied for development when it is desirable; revenues thus derived could in turn be used by counties to purchase land or development rights in areas not zoned agricultural, or to carry out other land use policies.

This use of the exchange principle in zoning should increase flexibility as well as providing greater equity. It takes the existing distribution of rights as given; those granted additional rights would pay for them, while those giving up rights would be compensated. It would allow counties to take advantage of the benefits involved in the rights they hold.

*This section based on William B. Lord, "Decision Making for Food Production," and Timothy D. Tregarthen, "Urbanizing Rural Land: Markets and Politics," papers prepared for the Food, Fuel, and Shelter Conference.

Fig. 6.1 Zoning, ownership (public or private) & lands platted*

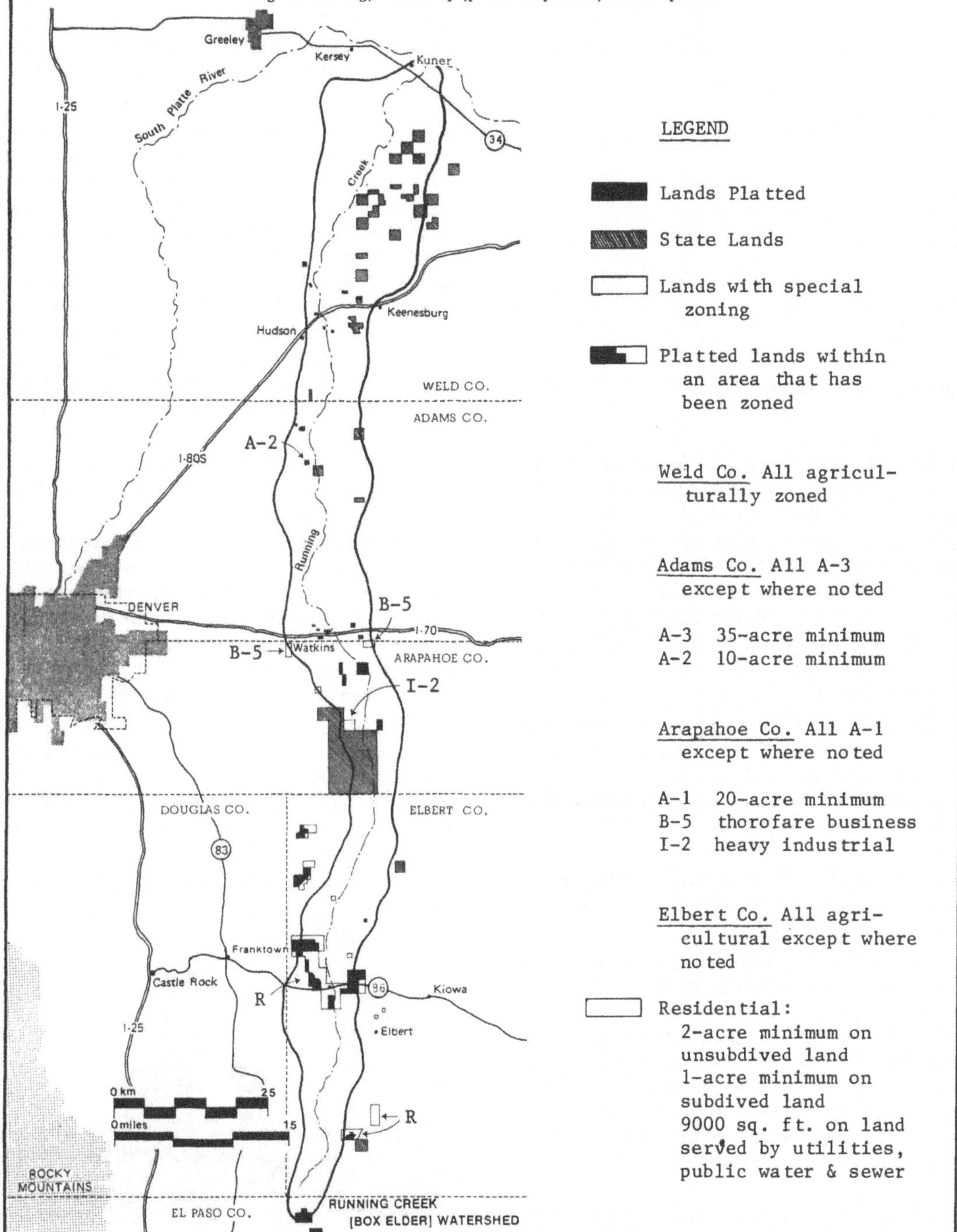

*as of May, 1976

Rights of Future Generations*

One critical feature of many land use decisions is their irreversible nature, at least over a fairly long span of time. Agricultural land that is urbanized cannot readily be converted back to agriculture. Coal taken from the Denver Basin and burned is gone. Decisions involving these resources involve effects over time as well as space. Future generations will thus be affected by present decisions. Should such generations have enforceable rights that should be considered in making these choices?

A "right" is a freedom to act in a particular way. Thus, rights for future generations might include the right to use Denver Basin coals. If such rights exist, it is reasonable to require that those who hold them wish to use them. This wish can be interpreted as an assumed wish based on a rational recognition of interests; this avoids the difficulty that future generations are unavailable to assert such wishes today.

One could test for the existence of a right using the criterion of whether that right is legally recognized; future generations would fare poorly in such a test for land use policy. But certainly one can distinguish moral rights from legal ones — there have, after all, been immoral laws. Thus a moral right may be held by future generations in the absence of, or reinforced by, a legal one. Note that there would be no particular legal problem in defining such rights. The absence of their holders from the present scene merely requires that some present person be designated as a guardian to speak on behalf of the holder of the right. In this same way, rights are currently defined for children, animals, ships, and corporations.

A right for one agent imposes a duty, or obligation, on another. Granting rights to future generations to Denver Basin coals imposes an obligation on the present generation not to exploit these coals. Are people willing to assume obligations on behalf of others? One can observe in human behavior a sympathy on the part of individuals for their fellow man. This sympathy is often manifested by charitable acts toward strangers. The limits of credibility are hardly strained by the supposition of a similar willingness to sacrifice now for a perceived plight of strangers to come. This willingness to sacrifice, to incur an obligation, defines the existence of a moral right.

The likelihood of this willingness to sacrifice for the future is increased when the nature of "future generations" is examined. Future generations — a few of them, anyway — will live along with somewhat older members of present generations. Further, the members of future generations will be the children, grandchildren, and so on, of people making decisions today. Willingness to sacrifice on behalf of one's own children is a widely held trait.

One can also defend the proposition that future generations have rights on grounds of fairness, that members of society have an implicit contract to treat other members fairly. Society can, of course, be defined over time to include future generations. A commonly accepted test of

Eldon Stevens

*This section based on: Eldon Stevens, "Do Future Generations Have Rights?" paper prepared for the Food, Fuel and Shelter Conference.

the fairness of a judgment is that the maker of the judgment would be willing to apply it to himself. Thus the "fair" amount of energy that the future individuals should have is the amount that present ones wish to have for themselves, recognizing this implicit obligation to share over time.

Whatever the justification of rights for future generations one wishes to establish, recognition of those rights will require present sacrifice. Coal saved for the future is coal given up now. Land use options such as transferring land from agriculture to urban use that are given up for the future are lost today. If present sacrifices are to be made, they must be justified — future generations must need them. Will future generations need Denver Basin coals? If one believes that solar energy will be widely — and relatively cheaply — available in 25 years, then present consumption of the coal is justified. Similarly, if one feels there will be plenty of food in the future, one need not worry about putting towns on agricultural land. Further, if the experience of the last few hundred years is an accurate guide, future generations will be richer; present sacrifice on their behalf would redistribute income from lower to higher income groups.

But these are uncertain prospects; the decisions based on them and on present and future generations are difficult ones indeed. Difficulty and uncertainty do not, however, obviate choice; decisions must be made. Recognition of possible needs of the future need not imply a grinding halt to the consumption of exhaustible resources and options, but it would slow the flow of land use out of agriculture on the watershed.

John Hand, R. James Nicholson

Conclusion

Food, fuel, and shelter needs present society with difficult choices. Increasing the information base on which they are made does not make the choices easier. Indeed, it probably makes them more difficult. But it should also make the choices that are made better ones. That way the real aim of the Food, Fuel, and Shelter Conference — to provide an information base on the nature of trade-offs in land use decisions that would improve those decisions would be achieved. More work (a list of important research needs follows) remains; that will always be the case. But decisions must be made in the meantime. It is therefore essential that the implications of these decisions be thought through as carefully as possible with the information at hand. If conferences such as the Food, Fuel, and Shelter Conference succeed in bringing decision makers together in such a problem solving focus, then they will continue to be worthwhile.

Some Topics for Further Research on the Watershed

One guide to future research needs is provided by the matrices discussed above. The relationships suggested by them need to be explored and, where possible, quantified. The list below seeks to expand on some of the questions raised in the trade-off matrices. No attempt has been made to arrange the research topics by order of priority.

*Effects of increasing climate variability on agricultural operations

*Prospects for controlled, intensive agriculture

*Effects of subdivision development on neighboring farms and ranches

*Relative importance of "psychological" vs. money income on decisions to hold land in agricultural use

*Effects of increased water prices on irrigated farms

*Role of animal life in agricultural operations

*Effects of rising energy prices on the mix of agricultural land uses, i.e. irrigated crops, dry land crops, and pasture

*The economic value of open space provided by agricultural operations

*Mechanisms to compensate farmers and ranchers for their provision of open space

*Economies of scale in agricultural operations

*Efficient grazing intensities under varying price, cost, and environmental conditions

*Economic base model of the region

*New employment sources possible on the watershed

*Techniques for assisting rural political jurisdictions in decision-making in the face of pressure for rapid growth

*Methods for cooperative agreements among political jurisdictions

*Reflecting state interests in local decisions

*Early warning systems for development pressures

*Effects of local tax regulatory structures on development

*The role of a watershed as a focus for land use planning

*Land use regulatory approaches available to government agencies

*Inventory of water rights held by watershed property owners and jurisdictions

*Demography of the watershed

*Effects of major energy development on local communities

*Distribution of costs in energy development

*Reclamation prospects for strip-mined land in a semi-arid environment

*The watershed as a corridor for the transmission of energy

*Prospects for alternative energy sources on the watershed

*Effects of food, fuel, and shelter development on animal life

*Relationships of watershed development to growth rates in Colorado Springs, Denver, and Greeley

*Flood control problems in watershed development

*Goals of watershed residents for future development patterns

*New design approaches for shelter needs on the watershed

*Key factors in siting decisions for developers

*Community values vis à vis needs of future generations

*Developing greater appreciation for grasslands landscapes

*Assessment of rights of established, new, and potential residents of communities

*Sharing the costs of urbanization in rural areas

*Human and natural history of the watershed

*Transferability of land use analyses among watersheds in general

APPENDIX A

PROGRAM

Thursday, May 20

8: 00 am Registration and distribution of information packets

9:00 am Welcome and Opening Remarks
Timothy Tregarthen, Conference Director

9: 15 am "The Front Range Piedmont: Pre-Critical Conditions on the High Plains"
Elizabeth Wright Ingraham, Director, Wright-Ingraham Institute

9: 55 am "Natural Systems of the Front Range"
George Van Dyne, Colorado State University

10:35 am "Institutional Arrangements"
Curtiss E. Frank Colorado State University

11:15 am BREAK

11:30 am "Land Use Programs, State of Colorado"
Philip Savage, Director, Colorado Land Use Commission

NOON Luncheon

1:00 pm WORKING GROUPS
Food Production
Energy Development
Urbanization

—participants are asked to work in one working group throughout the conference

3:30 BREAK

4:00 pm "Climate Conditions along the Front Range"
Thomas McKee, State Climatologist, Asst. Professor, Department of Atmospheric Science, Colorado State University

5:30 pm Cash bar

Watershed Forum

6: 00 pm Dinner & Speaker

Friday, May 21

8:00 am WORKING GROUPS RESUME

Food Production
Energy Development
Urbanization

11:00 am BREAK

NOON Luncheon

Watershed Forum

1:00 pm PANEL

"Critical Issues in Industry on the Watershed"
John Hand, Project Manager, Cameron Engineers, Inc., Denver
John Stencel, President, Rocky Mountain Farmers' Union
Representative Colorado Association for Housing and Building
Moderator, Eric D. Kelly, Rahenkamp, Sachs, Wells & Assoc., Denver and Philadelphia

2:30 pm WORKING GROUPS RESUME

5:00 pm Cash bar

6: 00 pm Dinner

Watershed Forum

7:30 pm Speaker, Beatrice E. Willard, Council on Environmental Quality, Washington D.C.

Saturday, May 22

8:00 am WORKING GROUPS RESUME (wrap-up session)

Watershed Forum

9:00 am SUMMARY SESSION

11:00 am Group discussions on how conference work might apply to areas outside of Running Creek (Box Elder) Watershed
Moderator, Terrill J. Minger, Manager, Town of Vail, Colorado

NOON Buffet Lunch

Conference end

Speakers being confirmed and will be announced

Watershed Tour

APPENDIX B

Participants in the Food, Fuel and Shelter Conference

Rodney Alt
USDA Soil Conservation Service
Greeley, Colorado

Mary Anderson
Town Clerk
Elizabeth, Colorado

Richard D. Andrews
Rocky Mountain Energy Company
Denver, Colorado

Susan Spitz Carmichael, Director
Colorado Humanities Program
Boulder, Colorado

Donald Crane (speaker)
Governor's Energy Policy Council
Denver, Colorado

Kenneth D'Appolonia
E. D'Appolonia Consulting Engineers, Inc.
Denver, Colorado

David Dechant
Ft. Lupton, Colorado

Nikki Dilgrade
Lakewood, Colorado

Stephen Dole
Cameron Engineers, Inc.
Denver, Colorado

Jeff Doose
Denver, Colorado

Brendan Doyle (Conference Coordinator)
Wright-Ingraham Institute
Colorado Springs, Colorado

Curtiss E. Frank, Ph.D. (speaker)
Sociology Department
Colorado State University
Ft. Collins, Colorado

John Hand (speaker)
Cameron Engineers, Inc.
Denver, Colorado

Roger Hein
Rocky Mountain Energy Company
Denver, Colorado

H. Kenneth Gayer, Ph.D.
Division of Advanced Environmental
Research and Technology
National Science Foundation
Washington, D.C.

Randy Herrick-Stare
(recorder Energy Div. Workshop)
Denver, Colorado

Victor Hornbein, Architect (Inv. Team)
Victor Hornbein & Associates
Denver, Colorado

Catherine Tobin Ingraham
Staff
Wright-Ingraham Institute
Colorado Springs, Colorado

Elizabeth Wright Ingraham
President
Wright-Ingraham Institute
Colorado Springs, Colorado

Eric Kelly (speaker)
Rahenkamp, Sachs, Wells & Assoc.
Denver, Colorado

Robert Krimmer
Pueblo Regional Planning Commission
Pueblo, Colorado

Ivo E. Lindauer, Ph.D.
Department of Biological Sciences
University of Northern Colorado
Greeley, Colorado

William Lord, Ph.D., Economics
(Investigatory Team)
Insititue of Behavorial Sciences
University of Colorado
Boulder, Colorado

Suzanne Lynch, Attorney
(recorder, Urbanization Workshop)
Denver, Colorado

Thomas McKee, Ph.D. (speaker)
State Climatologist
Colorado State University
Ft. Collins, Colorado

Alan Merson, LL.D.
(also Chmn. of State Land Use Commission
and member of Investigatory Team)
College of Law, University of Denver
Denver, Colorado

Frank Miller
Staff, Wright-Ingraham Institute
Colorado Springs, Colorado

James R. Miller
Land Use Administrator
Elbert County
Kiowa, Colorado

Terrill J. Minger
Town Manager
Vail, Colorado

R. James Nicholson, Attorney (speaker)
Colorado Association for Housing and
Building
Denver, Colorado

Sherry Oaks
(recorder, Food Production Workshop)
Vail, Colorado

Gayle Packard-Seeburger
Adams County Planning Department
Brighton, Colorado

Kathryn Pappenheim
(Secretary, Weld County Farmers Union)
Eaton, Colorado

Steve Peters
Ft. Collins, Colorado

Jesse E. Powers
Henderson, Colorado

John Ragsdale
Littleton, Colorado

Buford Rice
Colorado Farm Bureau
Denver, Colorado

John Stencel, President (speaker)
Rocky Mountain Farmers Union
Denver, Colorado

Eldon Stevens, Ph.D. Philosophy
(Investigatory Team)
University of Colorado
Colorado Springs, Colorado

Timothy Tregarthen, Ph.D. Economics
(Conference Director)
University of Colorado
Colorado Springs, Colorado

George M. Van Dyne, Ph.D. Ecology
(Investigatory Team)
Colorado State University
Ft. Collins, Colorado

Sallie Van Dyne
Bellevue, Colorado

James Veenstra
(Weld County Planning Dept. Intern)
Greeley, Colorado

David Ver Steeg
(Investigatory Team)
Environment Consultants, Inc.
Lakewood, Colorado

Eric Walther, Ph.D.
Charles F. Kettering Foundation
Dayton, Ohio

Dwight Whitney (1041 Representative)
Division of Planning
Department of Local Affairs
Denver, Colorado

John D. Winkel
Laramie, Wyoming

Eli Yakich, Jr.
Public Service Co. of Colorado
Denver, Colorado

APPENDIX C

METRIC MEASUREMENTS AND CONVERSION TABLES USED IN THIS REPORT

U.S. to METRIC

length

1 inch = 2.54 centimeters

1 foot = 0.3 meter (m)

1 mile = 1.6 kilometers (km)

area

1 acre = 0.4 hectare (ha)

1 square mile = 2.6 square kilometers (km^2)

mass

1 pound = 0.45 kilogram (kg)

1 ton (2,000 lbs.) = .907 metric tons

volume

1 bushel = .035 cubic meter (m^3)

temperature

(°F - 32) X 5/9 = °C

METRIC to U.S.

length

1 centimeter = .39 inches

1 meter (m) = 3.28 feet

1 kilometer (km) = 0.62 miles

area

1 hectare (10,000 square meters) = 2.47 acres

1 square kilometer = 0.39 square mile

mass

1 kilogram (kg) = 2.2 pounds

1 metric ton = 1.102 tons (short)

volume

1 cubic meter (m^3) = 28.38 bushels (dry)

temperature

(°C X 9/5) + 32 = °F

CONVERSION RATIOS

bushels/acre times .088 equals cubic meters/hectare

tons/acre times 1.13 equals metric tons/hectare

For example:

"30 bushel wheat" = 30 bushels/acre = 2.6 cubic meters/hectare

35 bushels/acre = 3.1 m^3/hectare

2.2 acres/heifer/month = .9 hectares/heifer/month

15-20 acres/year/animal = 6.8 hectares/year/animal

35 acres/year/animal = 14 hectares/year/animal

15-17 inches precipitation = 37.6 - 43.2 centimeters precipitation

32°F = 0°C

50°F = 10°C

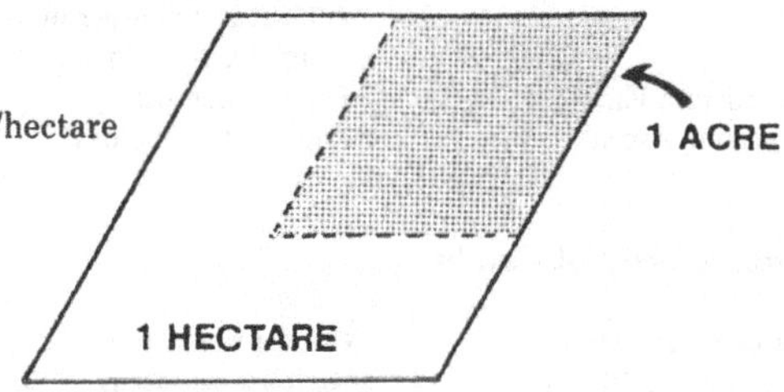

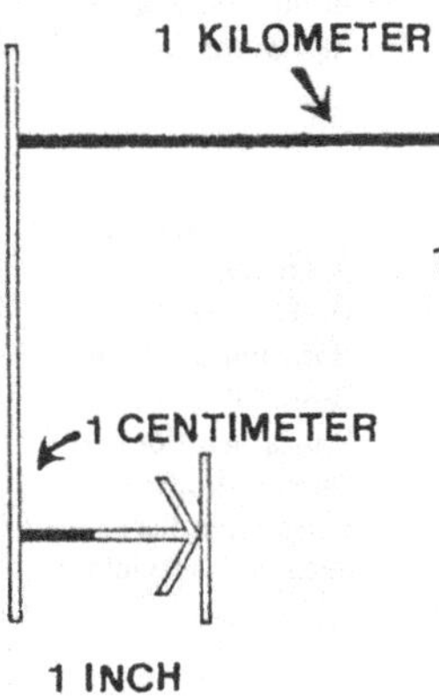

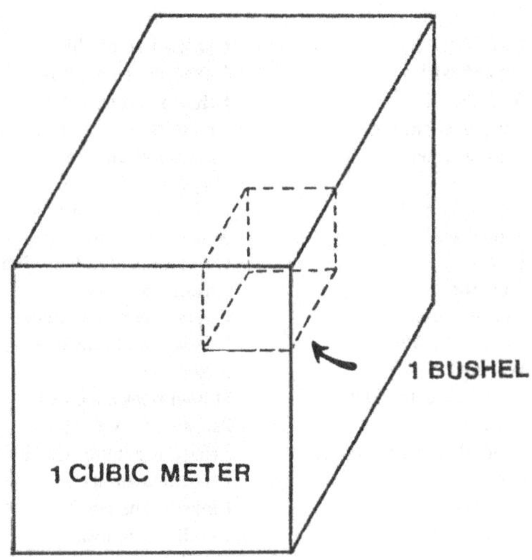

APPENDIX D

NAMES OF PLANTS CITED IN THIS REPORT

Trees

Cottonwood	Populus sargentii
Douglas fir	Pseudotsuga menziesii
Juniper	Juniperus communis
	Juniperus mexicana
	Juniperus monospermum
	Juniperus scopulorum
Ponderosa Pine	Pinus ponderosa
Quaking Aspen	Populus tremuloides

Shrubs and Half-shrubs

broom snakeweed	Gutierrezia sarothrae
four-wing saltbrush	Atriplex canescens
fringed sagewort	Artemisia frigida
Hippianna rose	Potentilla hippiana
mountain mahogany	Cercocarpus montanus
sand sagebrush	Artemisia filifolia
scrub oak	Quercus gambelii
wild rose	Rosa acicularis
winterfat	Eurotia lanata

Forbs

bull thistle	Cardus Leiophyllis
crownbeard	Verbesina encelioides
fleabane	Erigeron compositus
fringed wormwood	Artemisia dracunculoides
lambsquarter	Chenopodium album
locoweed	Oxytropis deflexa
mountain muhly	Mulenbergia montana
nightshade	Solanum americanum
pigweed	Cycloloma atriplicifolium
pussytoe	Antenaria rosea
rubber rabbitbrush	Chyrsothamus nauseosus
Russian thistle	Salsola kali tenuifolia
sagewort	Artemisia
scarlet globemellow	Sphaeralcea coccinea
scurfpea	Psoralea tenuiflora
slenderbrush eriogonium	Eriogonum microthecium
sunflower	Hilanthus annus
toadflax	Linaria canadensis
western yarrow	Achillea lanulosa

Grasses and Sedges

Tall Grasses and Sedges

big bluestem	Andropogon gerardii
Indian grass	Sorghastrum nutans
prairie dropseed	Sporobolus cryptandrus
switchgrass	Panicum virgatum

Midgrasses and Sedges

alkali sacaton	Sporobolus airiodes
Arizona fescue	Festuca arizonica
Bottle brush squirreltail	Stitanion longifloium
crested wheatgrass	Agropyron cristatum
green needlegrass	Stipa viridula
junegrass	Koeleria cristata
intermediate wheatgrass	Agropyron intermedium
Kentucky bluegrass	Poa pratensis
little bluestem	Andropogon scoparius
needle and thread	Stipa comata
needlegrass	Stipa neomexicana
nodding brome	Bromus porteri
prairie sandreed	Calamovilfa longifolia
pubescent wheatgrass	Agropyron trichophorum
red three-awn grass	Aristida longeseta
Russian wild rye	Andropogon hallii
sand dropseed	Sporobolus cryptandrus
side-oats grama	Bouteloua certipendula
smooth brome	Bromis inermis
western wheatgrass	Agropyron smithii

Shortgrasses and Sedges

blue grama	Bouteloua garcilis
hairy grama	Bouteloua hirsuta
inland saltgrass	Distichlis stricta
little barley	Hordeum pusillum
needleleaf sedge	Carex filifolia
six-week fescue	Vulpia octoflora
threadleaf sedge	Carex stenophylla
tumblegrass	Schedonnardus paniculatus
buffalograss	Buchloë dactyloides

BIBLIOGRAPHY

Auger, Camilla and Maurice, Raymond, "Socio-economic Assessment of Energy Development in Western Colorado," Appendix E1, *Future Energy Alternatives for Colorado*, Colorado Energy Research Institute, Golden, 1976.

Baumol, William, J., "Macroeconomics of Unbalanced Growth: The Anatomy of Urban Crisis," *American Economic Review*, 57, June 1967, pp. 413-426.

Bell, A.V., and D.R. Nancarrow, "Salmon and Mining in Northeastern New Brunswick," *CIM Bulletin*, v. 67, no. 751, 1974, pp. 44-53.

Bement, R.E. "Implementing Range Management," *Range Beef Cow Symposium*, Cheyenne, December 13-15, 1971, Proceedings pp. 95-97.

Ben David, Avrom, *Regional Analysis for Practitioners*, Revised Edition, Praeger, New York, 1974, pp. 82-93.

Bish, Robert, L., *The Public Economy of Metropolitan Areas*, Markham, Chicago, 1971.

Blanchet, K.A. Quesada, L. Erickson, B. Hendricks, P. Nalluswami, and E. Taylor, "An Abstract Bibliography on Shortgrass and Mixed Grass Prairie Ecosystems," *U.S. IBP Grassland Biome Study Technical Report* no. 236, Colorado State University, Fort Collins, 1973.

Bucyrus-Erie, "A Call for Action, U.S. Energy Independence by 1985," Federal Energy Administration Special Report.

Clawson, Marion, "Why not Sell Zoning (Legally That Is?)," *Cry California*, Winter, 1966-67, pp. 9-39.

Coleman, D.C., R. Andrews, J.E. Ellis, and J.S. Singh, "Energy Flow in Man-managed and Natural Ecosystems," ms., 1976. Agro-Ecosystems 3:45-54.

Conklin, Howard, E., et al, *Maintaining Viable Agriculture in Areas of Urban Expansion*, New York State Office of Planning Services: Albany, 1972, p. 29.

Costello, D.F. "Natural Revegetation of Abandoned Plowed Land in the Mixed Grass Prairie Association of Northeastern Colorado," *Ecology*, 25, 1974, pp. 312-326.

Council on Environmental Quality, *Environmental Quality, Sixth Annual Report*, Washington, D.C.: U.S. Government Printing Office, December 1975, p. 163.

Davis, Otto, "Economic Elements in Municipal Zoning Decisions," *Land Economics*, 39 (4), November 1963, pp. 375-386.

Dupree, Corsentino, "U.S. Energy through the Year 2000," Revised, *U.S. Bureau of Mines, Special Report*, 1974.

Energy Research and Development Administration: A National Plan for Energy Research, Development and Demonstration, Volume 1, ERDA 48, Washington, D.C., 1975.

Federal Energy Administration, Project Independence, Washington, D.C., November 1974.

Fish, E.B., "Seconday Succession on Upper Kiowa Creek Watershed," M.S. Thesis, Colorado State University, 1966.

Gilmore, John and Mary Duff, *Policy Analysis for Rural Development and Growth Management in Colorado*, Colorado Rural Development Commission, Denver, 1974.

Goldberg, Victor, "Toward an Expanded Theory of Contract," *Journal of Economic Issues*, 10 (1), March 1976, pp. 45-61.

Greb, B.W., D.E. Smika, N.P. Woodruff, and C.J. Whitfield, "Summer Fallow in the Great Plains," *USDA Conservation Research Report* 17, 1974, p. 5185.

Hebb, D.H., "Economic Impact of Alternative Energy Supply Policies in Colorado: A Summary Report," *Colorado School of Mines Mineral Industries Bulletin*, volume 16, 1975.

Heilbrun, James, *Urban Economics and Public Policy*, St. Martins Press, New York, 1974.

Hoffman, G.R., and G.J. Tomlinson, "A Bibliography of Vegetational Studies in Colorado," *Southwestern Naturalist* 11:228-237, 1977.

Hull, A.C., D.F. Hervey, C.W. Doran, and W.J. McGinnies, "Seeding Colorado Rangelands," *Colorado Agriculture Experiment Station Bulletin* 498-5, 1958.

Hyatt, D.E., "The Environmental Impact Statement: A New Requirement in Planning The Mining Operation," *Colorado School of Mines Mineral Industries Bulletin* volume 16, no. 3, 1973.

Hyder, D.N., R.E. Bement, E.E. Remmenga, and D.F. Hervey, "Ecological Responses of Native Plants and Guidelines for 1975, Management of Shortgrass Range," *USDA Technical Bulletin* 1503.

Ingraham, E.W., "Lead Time for Assessing Land Use: A Case Study," *Science*, 194:17-22, 1976.

Jameson, D.A., and R.E. Bement, "General Description of the Pawnee Site," *U.S. IBP Grassland Biome Study Technical Report* no. 1, Colorado State University, Fort Collins, 1969.

Johnson, W.M., "Natural Revegetation of Abandoned Cropland in the Ponderosa Pine Zone of the Pike's Peak Region in Colorado," *Ecology* 26: 363-374, 1945.

Kelly, J.M., G.M. Van Dyne, W.F. Harris, "Comparison of Three Methods of Assessing Grassland Productivity and Biomass Dynamics," *American Midland Naturalist* 92:357-369, 1974.

Klipple, G.E., and D.F. Costello, "Vegetation and Cattle Responses to Different Intensities of Grazing," 1960. (USDA Tech. Bulletin 1216).

Larsen, L.S., T.G. Barber, E.L. Wesswick, D.E. McCoy, and J.B. Harman, "Soil Survey Elbert County, Colorado — Eastern Part," *Soil Survey Series* 1960 no. 31, USDA, SCS, 1966.

Larsen, L.S., and J.B. Brown, *Soil Survey of Arapahoe County, Colorado*, USDA, SCS, 1971.

Larsen, L.S., *Soil Survey of Castle Rock Area, Colorado*, USDA, SCS.

Livingston, R.B., "An Ecological Study of the Black Forest, Colorado," *Ecological Monographs*, 19:123-144, 1949.

Marcus, Norman and Marilyn Groves et al., *The New Zoning: Legal Administrative and Economic Concepts and Techniques*, Praeger, New York, 1970.

McGinnies, D.J., D.F. Hervey, J.A. Downs, and A.C. Everson, "A Summary of Range Grass Seeding Trials in Colorado," *Colorado Agricultural Experiment Station Technical Bulletin* 73, 1963.

McHarg, Ian, "Where Should Highways Go?" *Landscape Architecture*, 1967, pp. 179-181.

McHarg, Ian, "A Comprehensive Highway Route Selection Method," *Highway Research Record* 246, Highway Research Board, Washington, D.C., 1968, pp. 1-15.

McHarg, Ian, *Design with Nature*, The Natural History Press, Garden City, New York, 1969.

Miller, C.A., "Regional Analysis and Management of Environmental Systems: Descriptions of Some Currently Available Resource Planning Tools," Department of Forest and Wood Science, Colorado State University, Fort Collins, 1969.

National Coal Association, *Coal Facts 1974-1975*, Washington, D.C.

Peterson, George and Harvey Yampolsky, "Urban Development and the Protection of Metropolitan Farmland," The Urban Institute, 1975.

P.U.C. Staff, "1975 Energy Report to the Commission," *Annual Report of the P.U.C.*, specific tables and charts, 1975.

Romero, J.C. and E.R. Hampton, Maps showing the approximate configuration and depth to the top of the Laramie-Fox Hills aquifer, U.S.D.I., Geological Survey, *Miscellaneous Geological Investigations*, Denver Basin, Colorado, Maps 1-791, plate 72.

Sampson, J.J., and J.G. Baber, *Soil Survey of Adams County*, Colorado, USDA, SCS, 1974, 72 p. and maps.

Shantz, H.L. "Natural Vegetation as an Indicator of the Capabilities for Crop Production in the Great Plains Area." *USDA Bureau of Plant Industry Bulletin* 201, 1911.

Singh, J.S. "Update of the U.S. IBP Grassland Biome Literature a KWIC Index and Abstract," *U.S. IBP Grassland Biome Study Technical Report* no. 245, Colorado State University, Fort Collins, 1974, 211 p.

Striffler, W.D. "Hydrological Data, 1970, Pawnee Grasslands," *U.S. IBP Grassland Biome Study Report* no. 75, Colorado State University, Fort Collins, 1971, 23p.

Swartzman, G.L., and G.M. Van Dyne, "An Ecologically Based Simulation-Optimization Approach to Natural Resource Planning," *Annual Review of Ecology and Systematics* 3:347-398, 1972.

Swartzman, G.L. and G.M. Van Dyne, "Land Allocation Decisions: A Mathematical Programming Framework Focusing on Quality of Life," *Journal of Environmental Management* 3:105-132, 1975.

Turner, A.K., "Computer Aided Environmental Impact Analysis, part 1, Procedures, *Colorado School of Mines Mineral Industries Bulletin*, 19, (2), 1976.

Turner, A.K., and D.M. Coffman, "Geology for Planning: A Review of Environmental Geology," *Colorado School of Mines Quarterly*, volume 68, no. 3, 1973.

Turner, G.T. and G.E. Klipple, "Growth Characteristics of Blue Grama in Northeastern Colorado," *Journal of Range Management* 5:22-28, 1952.

U.S. Department of Interior, "Coal Resources of the U.S., January 1, 1974," *U.S. Geological Survey Bulletin* 1412, 1975.

U.S. Department of the Interior, *Energy Prospectives: Presentation of Major Energy and Energy Related Data*, Washington, D.C., February 1975.

University of Oklahoma, *Energy Alternatives, a Comparative Analysis: Science and Public Policy Program*, Norman, Oklahoma, 1975.

Van Dyne, G.M., "A Systems Approach to Grasslands," International Grasslands Congress, Proceedings 11:A131-A143. This article also appears 89-101 in Daetz, D.R.H. Pantell et al., *Environmental Modelling: Benchmark Papers in Electrical Engineering and Computer Science*, Dowden, Hutchinson, and Ross, 1976.

Van Dyne, G.M., (Principal Investigator), *Analysis of Structure, Function and Utilization of Grassland Ecosystems, volume II, A Progress Report*, Colorado State University, 1971.

Van Dyne, G.M., "An Overview of the Ecology of the Great Plains Grasslands with Special Reference to Climate and its Impact," *U.S. IBP Grasslands Biome Study Technical Report* 290, Colorado State University, 1975.

Van Dyne, G.M., "Systems Analysis as an Approach to Grazing Land Problems and Research," 1975, pp. 78-80. In international working group on project three, "Impact of Human Activities and Land Use Practices on Grazing Lands: Savanna Grasslands (from Temperate to Arid Zones), Final Report, *Unesco MAB Report Series* no. 25, Paris, 1975.

Van Dyne, G.M., W.R. Keammerer, S.G. Martin, J. Merino, R. Porter, R.L. Stoecker, and M.J. Redding, "Evolving Conceptualization of Ecological Interrelationships on the c-b Tract, 1976, pp. 441-512. *In* c-b Shale Oil Project, Ashland Oil, Inc., and Shell Oil Co. Oil Shale Tract c-b, "First Year Environmental Baseline Program — Annual Summary and Trends Report," Published by c-b Shale Oil Project, (Shell Oil Co., Operator), 1700 Broadway, Denver, November, 1974 through October, 1975.

Van Haveren, B.P., "Soil Water Phenomena of a Shortgrass Prairie Site," *U.S. IBP Grassland Biome Study Technical Report* no. 247, Colorado State University, Fort Collins.

Weaver, J.E., and F.W. Albertson, *Grasslands of the Great Plains: Their Nature and Use*, Johnson Publications Company, Lincoln, Nebraska, 1956.

Whyte, William H. Jr., "Securing Open Space for Urban America: Conservation Easements," *Urban Land Institute Technical Bulletin* no. 36, Washington, D.C., December 1959, p. 8.

Williams, T.E. and Z.E. Holch, "Ecology of the Black Forest of Colorado," *Ecology* 27:139-149, 1946.

Wiseman, Clark, "Land Zoning Changes: An Economic Perspective," *The Rocky Mountain Social Science Journal*, 12 (2), April 1975, pp. 59-68.

GLOSSARY

biomass (biology) is the dry weight of living matter, including stored food present in a species population expressed in terms of a given area or volume of a habitat.

carnivore (zoology) is an animal that eats flesh and subsists from animal protoplasm.

consumer (ecology) is an organism in an ecosystem which feeds on other organisams. A primary consumer, such as a herbivore, obtains its nutrition directly from plants; a secondary consumer, such as a carnivore, obtains its energy indirectly by feeding upon herbivores.

conglomerate (geology) is cemented, rounded fragments or waterworn rocks or pebbles bound by a siliceous or argilaceous substance.

drought (climatology) is a period of abnormally dry weather sufficiently prolonged so that the lack of water causes a serious hydrological imbalance (such as crop damage, water supply shortage) in the affected area; in general, the term should be reserved for relatively extensive time periods.

fledgling (zoology) is a bird lacking adult plumage which is not yet able to fly.

food chain (ecology) is the scheme of feeding relationships by crop levels which unites the member species of a biological community.

forb (botany) is an herb other than a grass or a sedge.

growing season is the length of time between the last 0°C temperature observed in spring and the first 0°C temperature in the fall.

habitat (ecology) is the part of the physical environment in which a plant or animal lives.

herb a seed plant that lacks a persistent, woody stem above-ground and dies at the end of the season.

herbivore (zoology) is an animal that eats only vegetation.

invertebrate (zoology) is an animal lacking a backbone and internal skeleton.

microfauna (zoology) are microscopic animals; (ecology) are the fauna of a microhabitat.

microflora (botany) are microscopic plants; (ecology) are the flora of a microhabitat.

midgrasses (range sciences) is a qualitative term referring to grasses 30 to 60 centimeters in height in a normal year.

net primary productivity (ecology) is the total quantity of photosynthesizing organisms produced per unit-time in a specified habitat.

photosynthesis (biochemistry) is the synthesis of chemical compounds in light, especially the manufacture of organic compounds from carbon dioxide and a hydrogen source, such as water, with simultaneous liberation of oxygen, by chlorophyll containing plant cells.

plant community (ecology) is a grouping of plants growing together in a specific locality subjected and adapted for life under common conditions.

phenology (climatology) is the differing timing of the growth stages of a plant species e.g. lilac leaves appear in April, buds appear in May, flower in June, new seeds in August and then the lilac plant is dormant in December.

plant succession (ecology) is a gradual process brought about by the change in number of individuals of each species of a community and by the establishment of a new species population which may gradually replace the original inhabitants.

raptorial birds (zoology) are predatory birds, such as eagles, hawks and owls, adapted for seizing or tearing their prey, e.g. claws and beaks.

scavenger (zoology) is an organism that feeds on carrion, refuse and similar matter.

secondary grasses (range sciences) characterize or typify the development of successional plant communities.

shortgrasses (range sciences) is a qualitative term referring to grasses 20 to 30 centimeters in height in a normal year.

semi-arid climate (climatology) is the type of climate in which precipitation, though very slight, is sufficient for growth of short, sparse grass.

tall grasses (range sciences) is a qualitative term referring to grasses above 60 centimeters in height in a normal year.

up-slope condition is an easterly flow of air into the foothills area or across the plains as it rises in elevation.

vertebrate (zoology) is the major subphylum of the phylum Chordata including all animals with backbones, from fish to man.

*All terms unless otherwise indicated, are taken from the Dictionary of Scientific and Technical Terms, McGraw-*Hill, Inc. 1974

Each definition is identified with the field of science or technology in which it is primarily used.

INDEX

This book was set in Century type by CV Composition and The Letter Setters.

For Product Safety Concerns and Information please contact our EU representative GPSR@taylorandfrancis.com Taylor & Francis Verlag GmbH, Kaufingerstraße 24, 80331 München, Germany

Batch number: 10748894

Printed by Printforce, the Netherlands